MURTY CLASSICAL
LIBRARY OF INDIA

MIR TAQI MIR
GHAZALS

MIR TAQI MIR

GHAZALS
Translations
of
Classic Urdu Poetry

Translated by
SHAMSUR RAHMAN FARUQI

MURTY CLASSICAL LIBRARY OF INDIA
HARVARD UNIVERSITY PRESS
Cambridge, Massachusetts
London, England
2 0 2 2

First published in Murty Classical Library of India,
Volume 21, Harvard University Press, 2019.

SERIES DESIGN BY M9DESIGN
TYPESETTING BY TITUS NEMETH

Library of Congress Cataloging-in-Publication Data

Names: Mīr, Mīr Taqī, -1810, author. |
Fārūqī, Shamsurraḥmān, 1935- translator. |
Container of (expression): Mīr, Mīr Taqī, -1810. Poems.
Selections. English. |
Container of (expression): Mīr, Mīr Taqī, -1810. Poems. Selections.
Title: Selected ghazals and other poems / Mir Taqi Mir ;
translated by Shamsur Rahman Faruqi.
Other titles: Murty classical library of India ; 21.
Description: Cambridge, Massachusetts : Harvard University Press, 2019. |
Series: Murty classical library of India ; 21 |
In English. |
Includes bibliographical references.
Identifiers: LCCN 2018030129 |
ISBN 9780674268753 (pbk.)
Classification: LCC PK2198.M49 A2 2019 | DDC 891.4/3913—dc23
LC record available at https://lccn.loc.gov/2018030129

CONTENTS

INTRODUCTION *vii*

GHAZALS *1*

NOTES *169*
GLOSSARY *183*
BIBLIOGRAPHY *185*

INTRODUCTION

Mir's Life

Muhammad Taqi, who later earned lasting renown as the great Urdu poet Mir Taqi Mir, or Muhammad Taqi Mir, or just Mir, was born in Agra (better known at that time in official and literary circles as Akbarabad) in September 1723. He died in Lucknow on September 10, 1810.[1]

Mir's ancestors came from the Hijaz in the Arabian Peninsula in the early 1600s. Some members of the family settled in Ahmedabad, and some traveled to Agra. His grandfather rose to be commander (or deputy commander) of a fort near Agra. His father, Muhammad Ali, had a son by his first wife, and at her death he contracted a second marriage. Mir was born from this union. Muhammad Ali was a strong believer in Sufism. In his autobiography, Mir eulogizes his father's spiritual status and attainments. Apparently he was named Ali Muttaqi (Ali, the God-fearing and pious) by one of his spiritual guides or friends.

Mir's father died in 1733. Mir's older half brother was cold and unhelpful, obliging Mir to seek his fortunes in Delhi (in 1734–1735), where he met with the distinguished nobleman Amir al-Umara Samsam al-Daula through a friend of his father's. Amir al-Umara granted a suitable pension to Mir, and, armed with the resources for a comfortable life, Mir returned to Agra to pursue his studies. The pension continued until Amir al-Umara's death in battle in 1739, when once again Mir became friendless and devoid of financial means.

He was obliged to return to Delhi to find employment or patronage.

Mir arrived in Delhi at the end of 1739 and lived in the house of the famous lexicographer, linguist, and Persian poet Siraj al-Din 'Ali Khan Arzu. Popularly known as Khan-e Arzu, he was the brother of Mir's stepmother. Relations between the two soured, though the reason for the rift is unknown. It is possible that Mir, who apparently had an early inclination to Shi'ism, became a full-fledged Shi'a around early 1741, and this may have caused their estrangement.

Mir's life from 1741 to 1782 was one of great literary success, though with its share of disputes and controversies and employment uncertainties. He sought, gained, and lost patrons due to the vicissitudes of life. Much of his employment was of a scholarly or diplomatic kind. He was never employed as an *ustad,* or literary mentor, by noblemen, which was a common practice at that time. In one case, he flatly refused a prominent nobleman's request to be his mentor because he did not find his poems "worthy of correction."[2]

Mir seems to have been essentially unemployed between the years 1772/1773 and 1780/1781. His wife died around 1771; nothing is known of his firstborn, a son called Faiz Ali, beyond the fact that he was a minor poet and died in 1808. Mir also had a daughter called Begam (this may have been her pen name); she too was a poet, but nothing else is known of her life, except that she was married to a nephew of Mir's and died in 1807.

Mir compiled his first poetry collection (*divan*) some time in the early 1750s, certainly before 1752. Around 1752, he composed in Persian his account of Rekhta (early Urdu) poets. He called it *Nikāt al-Shu'arā* (Subtle Points About Poets), and also included a brief literary credo and a definition of Rekhta poetry. In 1761/1762 he composed in Persian a short book of tales about the Sufis. It was called *Faiẓ-e Mīr* (Mir's Bounty), and its ostensible purpose was the mental and moral education of his son, Faiz Ali. Mir's second poetry collection can be dated to around 1775/1776. By this time, he had also compiled a Persian collection. Mir may have begun (and even completed) a first draft of *Ẓikr-e Mīr,* his putative autobiography, in 1773. He continued to make small but significant changes and minor additions until 1788. I say "putative" because it is an autobiography only in name, though he claimed that it contained his "story" and the "events" of his life. Even so, it is the first autobiography by an Urdu poet, and among the very few written by premodern Persian or Urdu poets. During this time he also wrote Urdu poetry and was prolific in all the popular genres.

In early 1782, Asaf al-Daula, the Nawab of Awadh (r. 1775–1797), invited Mir to move to Lucknow. He arrived there sometime in April 1782, was presented to the nawab, and was enrolled among the poets at the court. He remarried at this point and had another son. The son, called Mir Kallu (this was probably his pet name, but no formal name has come down to us), was a considerable poet. His pen name was 'Arsh.

Mir's third, fourth, fifth, and sixth collections were compiled at Lucknow between the years 1785 and 1808. The third is substantial and contains a good bit of poetry composed in Delhi and elsewhere. The remaining were progressively shorter. It seems that, gradually, Mir grew frail and lacked the mental application for writing extensively. The high quality of the poetry, however, the tone of voice, and the favorite themes all remain unchanged from the first to the last.

There is a story that toward the end of Mir's life the College of Fort William in Calcutta (now Kolkata) invited him to a lectureship there but he refused. According to another story, the English governor general, or other Company dignitaries, invited him to visit their camp when they came to Lucknow. Mir refused, saying, "There can only be two things that might qualify me to visit with the Sahib: one is my lineage [as a Sayyid], but it can mean nothing to him; the other is my poetry, which he cannot understand. So what's the point of my making his acquaintance?"

Both stories may well be true, given Mir's proud and haughty temperament. So, too, may be the story narrated by poet and scholar Mirza 'Ali Lutf, a contemporary of Mir's, in his biographical dictionary of Urdu poets. According to Lutf, Mir is supposed to have appeared before a team of interviewers from the College of Fort William, who visited Lucknow to recruit faculty. Mir was rejected because he was found to be too old and frail.[3]

Very nearly all Mir anecdotes present him as haughty, forthright, and conscious of his dignity as a Sayyid and his status as a major poet. Although his claims to being a Sayyid are somewhat shaky, in his poetry Mir often insists on his Sayyid roots, so much so that this claim has become part of the Mir lore.

Mir's *Kulliyāt* (Collected Poems) was published by the College of Fort William in 1811, setting perhaps the final seal of authority on his position as the major poet of the time.

The Myths of Mir

Mir seems to have led an average eighteenth-century Indo-Muslim life in Northern India. The only exceptional aspect of his life was the fact that, because he was a prominent poet employed often by important noblemen, he saw more of politics and traveled more (though never very far from Delhi) than most educated Muslims of good family in those times. Unfortunately, a fiction about Mir's life led to a stereotypical assumption in Mir criticism. The fiction is that Mir's life was an unrelieved tale of misery and sorrow. The assumption is that his poetry is the true and consistent expression of this misery. The fiction became possible because of the belief, promoted by colonial educators in the late nineteenth century, that poetry should be the expression of personal emotional states and should be "true" and "natural." A very firm foundation of both beliefs was laid by *Āb-e Ḥayāt* (Water of Life), an account of Urdu "poets of renown" by Muhammad Husain Azad. Here is a sample:

The blossom of delight, or the spring of luxury and pleasure, or the joy of success and union never fell to the lot of Mir sahib. He just went on narrating the sad story of calamity and the sorrow of his ill luck which had been the portion that he brought with him from the time of his birth. And these [accounts] still affect the hearts and cause pain in the breast. This is because such themes were purely imaginary for other poets, but were true to his own state. Even his themes of [erotic] loving were used up in the garb of failure [in love and life], weeping and lamenting, unfulfilled desire and disappointment and separation from the loved one. His poetry speaks clearly and aloud that the heart from which I emanate wasn't just pain and sorrow personified, but it was the very bier [on which was laid the corpse] of unfulfillment and anguish.[4]

This tone is symptomatic of the colonial comprador understanding of premodern Urdu poetry, which was such that no substantial account of the *total* poetry of Mir could be produced by scholars and critics, Indian or Western. Whatever partial accounts there have been revolve around the myth of Mir rather than the reality of Mir.

The modern Urdu scholar Ralph Russell, better informed than most, chose to read Mir primarily as a poet of "illicit love." The bawdiness, the eroticism, the pain and the enjoyment of life, the clear and numerous instances of homosexuality (whether purely in conformity with contemporary literary conventions or possibly in reference to real-life relationships), the prominence and variety of Sufi themes, the close and wise observation of the world, the insistence on man's dignity and humanity—themes with which Mir's poetry abounds—did not count as genuine Mir. Russell went so far as to say that in the then-prevalent environment of religious rigor, even the Sufi's love of God counted as "illicit love."[5]

Lingering angst about such matters has also led some of Mir's modern editors to censor the poet's work. For instance, Urdu's greatest critic, Muhammad Hasan Askari, placed Mir far above his younger contemporary Ghalib (d. 1869), but his reasons were nonliterary. In his influential and otherwise excellent selection from Mir, he scrupulously avoided all the verses that hinted, even metaphorically or by way of literary convention, at homosexuality. Prominent progressive poet and critic Ali Sardar Ja'fari, in his selection of Mir, excised not only all the references to homosexuality but also verses on erotic themes.

The story of the maltreatment of Mir and his poetry would not be complete without mention of the myth of his style: Mir's style is simple; his verses are easy to understand because they don't have the complicated depths of Ghalib; his poetry "arises from the heart and falls upon the heart" (this is a translation of a Persian saying that was often invoked for Mir).

Another lasting myth about Mir is the uneven quality of his poetry. A misquoted remark from the nineteenth-century poet and influential literary personality Mustafa Khan Shefta lent powerful support to its wide circulation. According to the quotation, Shefta supposedly claimed, "His low was exceedingly low and his high was extremely high." Shefta said no such thing. In fact, he was criticizing some people for saying unfair things about Mir's famous contemporary Mirza Muhammad Rafi Sauda; Shefta goes on to cite an example of fair criticism by Sadr al-Din Khan Azurda in his biographical dictionary and selections from the poets. There, Azurda says the following about Mir: "Though his low is a little low, yet his high is very high."[6]

The false notion about Mir's unevenness had two effects. It has resulted in an emphasis on selected rather than collected editions of his poems, and in selections that are arbitrary or (at best) idiosyncratic. Given that his poetry was full of highs and lows, the logic went, it would be difficult if not impossible to read him in his entirety; he deserved a selection where his best poetry would be easily available. It can be safely said that there are few people today who have read Mir's collected poetry from cover to cover.

Mir's Artistry: The Ghazals

It will be useful to place Mir in a broader literary context, that of the Persian *ghazal* as produced in India from the mid-sixteenth to the mid-nineteenth century, in the so-called fashionable *sabk-e hindi,* or "Indian style," with a preference for, among other things, abstract themes, remote and far-fetched images, complexity of thought, and a strong predilection for metaphor. At that time, the *ghazal* was the most popular form for courtly and Sufi poetry, and as Persian ceded its place to Urdu in the eighteenth and nineteenth centuries, many of its poetic conventions and practices became part of Urdu literary culture. Mir, writing his *Nikāt al-Shu'arā* (Subtle Points About Poets), a short biographical dictionary of the poets, described Urdu poetry as "poetry in the manner of Persian poetry, in the language of the Exalted City of Shahjahanabad, Dihli."⁹ Mir was not a formal disciple to anyone in the art of Urdu or poetry, but his immediate influence was certainly Vali Dakani, who was stylistically part of an earlier period of Urdu poetry that had flourished in Gujarat and the Deccan, with a greater proportion of Indic vocabulary and imagery. Vali's poetry became the rage in Delhi around 1720, but soon after there was a turn to a more purely Persianized style of writing among north Indian poets.

In Vali's *ghazals,* the beloved is occasionally female, often male, and in many cases indeterminate. As a result, the notion—articulate or inarticulate—of the protagonist or the speaker in the poem becomes more important than any particular or actual identity. The protagonist-lover could now be an ideal lover whose gender is less important than the ideas expressed through the poem. The beloved also became a notion, an ideal, expressed and realized in the poem through metaphorical constructs. The beloved was no more an actual woman, man, or boy than the lover was an actual woman or man. Ultimately, the convention of an "idealized" rather than an "actual" lover-beloved relationship freed the poet from the demands of "reality" or "realism." As a result, love poetry in Urdu from the last quarter of the seventeenth century onward consists mostly, if not entirely, of "poems about love" and not "love poems" in the Western sense of the term. This is true of almost all of Indian-style Persian poetry too, and even of much other Persian poetry from earlier times.

The distinction between poet—the person who actually wrote the poem—and protagonist—the person, or the voice, that articulated the poem—was nowhere so seriously adduced and practiced as in the Indian-style Persian poetry and in Urdu love poetry of the eighteenth century. Since the *ghazal* was intended for recitation at literary salons and public gatherings, and was in any case largely disseminated by word of mouth, the whole proposition of the *ghazal* as a personal, private, no-audience-assumed text becomes ridiculous. The *ghazal's* association with oral performance had other important consequences. One is that, while a *ghazal* may be expressive of "emotions," in the ordinary sense of the term, these are not necessarily the poet's personal emotions. Poems needed to make sense of the experience, or the idea, of love, and in terms that made sense to the audience as a whole, rather than to a specific individual, beloved, or friend.

There are other literary features crucial to the *ghazal* form that need to be briefly addressed. The distinction between *ma'nī āfrīnī* (creation of meanings, that is, meanings that are implicit, or obliquely suggested, or multiple meanings) and *mazmūn āfrīnī* (creation of new themes) led to the recognition that there was a universe of discourse particular to the *ghazal*. Certain kinds of *mazmūns* were admissible in this universe of discourse; others were not. Thus while *mazmūns* were in theory infinite, each *mazmūn* had to have affinity with other *mazmūns* before it could be considered a proper subject for poetry. Therefore, one major convention—common, by the way, to Sanskrit, Indian-style Persian poetry, and Indian-style Turkish poetry—was that *mazmūns,* even words and images already used, should be reused, though in a new way, or with a new slant. Personal or personalized narration was by no means barred, but was not to be encouraged, and preferred only when it made sense in more general terms. One of the recurrent themes in the eighteenth-century Urdu *ghazal* is the poet's self-denigration as a mere "writer of elegies," and not of poems proper.

Certain themes occur again and again: dying at the hands of the beloved; shedding tears of blood; weeping tears so copious as to produce a devastating flood; the cruelty of the beloved; wandering far and away in a forest or wilderness; madness and all its attendant consequences caused by the beloved's cruelty, or intensity of passion, or alienation from friends and society; doing physical injury to oneself (though never suicide) out of desperation, or frenzy, or the desire to do something; ripping off one's clothes, especially the collar and the hem; separation, which is mostly involuntary on the lover's part, and very often because of the beloved deliberately neglecting or even severing connection with the lover; love as imprisonment or a state of being caged like a bird. These metaphors emerged from a particular theory of figuration, not recognized in Western poetics and not quite articulated in Urdu or Persian either. According to this theory, poetry was a quest for themes. Love was just another theme, not an event in the poet's real life; it also happened to be the most important theme for the *ghazal.* Moreover, the core function of love was to soften the heart, to make it receptive to more pain, which ultimately made the human heart receptive to the divine light. Pain, and things that caused pain, had a positive value. The lover's place was to suffer; the beloved's function was to inflict suffering. This was a Sufi formulation, but was regularly taken by the *ghazal* poet to be true in the *ghazal* universe. All this was a *mazmūn* for Urdu love poetry in the eighteenth century. The poet also suffered pain in search of *mazmūns*. Or he wept for a *mazmūn* that was lost, or couldn't be realized, or was experienced for a moment, and then lost.

In Mir's poetry, the Indian style is not immediately discernible. This is because Mir also possessed the quality of *kaifiyat*, which may be loosely described as mood. More accurately described, it is a quality that gives poetry an emotional power and appeal, to which the actual content or even the meaning of the poem may be largely irrelevant. While creation of meanings and creation of new themes are ideas that can be found—though not necessarily expressed in those exact terms—in the writings of the Indo-Persian poets of the seventeenth and the eighteenth centuries, *kaifi-yat* is a term not found in the Persian texts; it seems to have come into vogue in Urdu in the early eighteenth century. Its origin may be in Sanskrit *rasa* (aesthetic emotion) theory, but no direct or even indirect link has been found so far (or, to be more accurate, no research has been undertaken in that direction). It is possible that the punning characteristic of nineteenth-century Urdu poetry may have been inspired by Sanskrit, too. The use of this poetic figure (termed *śleṣa* in Sanskrit) in the Indo-Persian tradition dates back to the classical Persian poet Amir Khusrau (d. 1325), who boasted that he had composed verses that had as many as seven meanings.[10]

Creation of meanings and of new themes primarily involves the intellect and what Coleridge called the "esemplastic power of imagination," that is, a power that "dissolves, diffuses, dissipates, in order to recreate."[11] *Kaifiyat* does not depend on these elements. Poems with *kaifiyat* would rarely have what in a contemporary idiom might be called a surplus of meaning, or "the overflowing of the signifier by the signified."[12] Mir's achievement, rarely equaled and never surpassed, is that many of his *ghazal* verses are brimming with emotional affect and, at first glance, do not seem to be *saying* much. An expert or close reader would, however, soon find that more has been said in the poem than is apparent on the surface.

The lover-protagonist and the beloved-object both live in a world of extremes: supreme beauty, supreme cruelty, supreme devotion—all things are at their best, or worst, in this world. The beloved-object is not a passive recipient of the lover-protagonist's tribute of love, or a helpless nonentity, unable to alleviate the lover's pain or ameliorate the lover's condition. The beloved's "cruelty" may be real, or a metaphor for indifference or physical distance from the lover. But the indifference of the beloved is an active stance; it makes a point. The lover-protagonist would prefer death at the hands of the beloved to indifference. Death at the hands of the beloved—should one find oneself to be lucky enough to be killed in this way—carried degrees of merit and distinction. The lover-protagonist is the only true lover: all the rest are false, and given to lust, rather than desire, or love. This poetry is thus quite naturally more occupied with dying than most love poetry in other cultures. It reverberates throughout with the terror and the ecstasy of dying. Death, in spite of all its uncertainty and unfamiliarity, is an achievement, a respite, a transition. It thus follows that the lover-protagonist who survives seeks suffering and ill luck, disapproval of the worldly, loss of honor and station. Madness and banishment, or imprisonment, or general ill fame are the functions of true love: the stronger the madness, the farther the wandering, the blacker the infamy, the truer and deeper the love. All this is often expressed with the subtlest of wordplay, in the most vigorously metaphorical language, and, occasionally, with extremely vivid but generally noncarnal realizations of the beloved's body.

The only items somewhat firmly anchored in quotidian, recognizable reality are the "others"—friends, advisers, preachers, censors, the devout, and the priestly. None of these wish, on principle, to see the lover's life thrown away or faith destroyed by following the course of love rather than that of the world and of God as seen by the worldly and the priestly. The lover rarely listens to them, and generally holds them in contempt, regarding them as benighted, materialistic, and mundane, having no understanding of the inner life. The phrase *ahl-e zāhir* (the people of the obvious and apparent) sums it all up. The world of the *ghazal* is one where the outsider is the hero, where nonconformism is the creed, and where prosperity is poverty.

In spite of its idealistic and unworldly aura, the poetry of the *ghazal* also has an air of delight: the joy of making up poems with words, of making language strain at its limits and yet remain *ravānī* (flowing, felicitous, smooth in reciting, easy to remember). All *ghazal* poets, even in conventionally sad narration, employ wordplay to the best of their ability. As central as the restraint in the description of physicality is the exuberance in verbal execution in the best Urdu love poetry of the eighteenth century. Poets knew that wordplay infuses new life into old themes, expands the horizon of meaning, and often creates a tonal ambiguity that enriches the total feel of the poem. Their primary concern is to renew and refashion the language, thereby demonstrating and realizing its potential. Intertextuality, imagination, audience expectation: all play their part.[13]

Among Urdu poets, Mir is unique in his ability to produce *ghazals* full of *kaifiyat* and meaning, as well as *ravānī;* this alone should suffice to secure his reputation. Although not fond of cerebral and abstract themes, Mir sometimes produced verse that seems to anticipate Ghalib, the most cerebral and abstraction-loving of Urdu and Indo-Persian *ghazal* poets. As I hope the *ghazals* in this selection will show, Mir is one poet who can be Shakespearean without trying to be. Just as everything came naturally to Shakespeare, so it did to Mir. He was a poet who could justly claim to have been everywhere and seen everything.

The Translation

All translations are as literal as practically possible. Since many of the verses carry more meanings or suggestions than the one visible on the surface, I have tried to bring out in the translation the meaning or suggestion most amenable to modern idiomatic English. Similarly, there are some grammatical-rhetorical devices (especially the rhetorical-interrogative and subjunctive-exclamative) that are potent tools for the poet. Urdu, even everyday Urdu, uses these devices without inhibition. In poetry, they almost always enhance or expand the meaning. Such devices are most often not available to modern English and sound forced and stilted even when rendered in English with care. I have used them as rarely as possible. In a formally structured *ghazal*, one line of verse consists actually of two more or less independent hemistichs or lines, each called a *misra'*. Ordinarily, a *misra'* of Urdu verse (especially in the *ghazal*) contains no more than seven to ten words, but most of them are so charged with meaning (conventions, literary culture, polysemy) and have so much else besides by way of associations and a rich hinterland of meaning generated by centuries of past usage, that an adequate English rendering (if at all possible) may demand many more than the normal seven-ten words for each line.

Each *ghazal* has been translated in full. No verse has been omitted on grounds of what some critics might consider lack of quality, untranslatability, or unsuitability (for whatever reason, including the tastes of the modern English speaker). Given the nature of the genre and the literary culture that produced it, all the verses in a given *ghazal* may not be of equally high literary quality. Conventional Urdu criticism has long held that Mir's poetry is extremely uneven—a good or even great verse can be preceded or followed by numerous "bad" ones. This is far from the truth, but we must bear in mind that even the apparently "inferior" verses must always have, and certainly in the case of a great poet like Mir do have, some piquant point, some subtle linguistic merit, which may not be always obvious upon first reading. It is inevitable that such felicities will be lost to the reader in translation, but I have made my best effort to hint at them, if not actually reproduce them in English, with due and paramount regard to comprehensibility in translation.

In spite of the stress on literalness, I have respected the integrity of the English language as spoken and written today and have avoided archaisms. Some exceptions, though very few, have been made in the interest of authenticity. A notable example is *jigar,* which means "liver." It was as much a seat of love, courage, and passion as *dil* (heart). In premodern Urdu and Persian poetry, and in modern Urdu poetry even, they are often interchangeable. Since up to the seventeenth century in English, too, the liver was regarded, like the heart, as the seat of love and violent passion and courage, I have translated the Urdu *jigar* as "liver" where the text has both "heart" and "liver" in the same verse. In other places, I have translated *jigar* as "heart" unless the meaning demands something different.

Though not an archaism, another word whose translation has caused me to make compromises is *hijr,* "separation." But "separation" in modern English carries so much socio-legal load that it can barely serve to convey the meaning of *hijr,* which in Urdu is almost always involuntary and never a socio-legal activity. In Urdu, the sense of *hijr* that is uppermost is "the state of being alone, away from the beloved."

It often occurs as counterpoint to *vasl/visāl,* meaning "joining, meeting, uniting," and so forth. But in Urdu poetry, *vasl* always means "sexual union," and *visāl* has the same connotation, except that in formal Urdu, *visāl* means "death, especially of a holy and venerable person."[14] One could use "union" for *vasl/visāl,* but the opposite, "disunion," though good English, does not have the desired resonance of loving, physical distance, and pain. I have been obliged to use different words and phrases to connote the sense of "disunion," including, occasionally, "disunion" itself.

Notes have been provided wherever considered absolutely essential. However, it is possible that some readers may find many more points needing assistance—something I could not fairly determine. Grateful acknowledgment is made here to Frances Pritchett, who has provided additional notes and a comprehensive glossary as per her own perception of potential reader needs.

The Order of the Poems

The order of the *ghazals* is arbitrary, except the two placed first and the one placed last. This has been done advisedly. The first two, though by no means chronologically the two earliest or latest, serve to give a very general idea of the kind of poet that the reader may expect to encounter in the ensuing pages. The last, again by no means the last *ghazal* composed, may be regarded as the poet's parting and prophetic words.

I translated the *ghazals* as I read and reread the whole corpus, and chose during each reading what struck me as suitable, from the point of view of general excellence and translatability. The present selection is the fruit of many readings carried out with the specific view of producing a worthwhile compendium of Mir's poetry in English.

As there was originally no logic or system in arranging the *ghazals* in the *Collected Poetry of Mir*, or his *Kulliyāt*, (where they were listed in order of the letters of the Urdu alphabet, but within a particular letter not ordered in any particular way), it was unnecessary to follow any particular sequence. The order of the *ghazals* here is simply the order in which I have translated them.

It must be remembered that poets in those days collected their *ghazals* without regard to date of composition, or their putative excellence, or the poet's or his patron's preference. Since each verse in a *ghazal* almost always stands alone and has no connection or relevance to what came before or after it, the question of imposing any external order on the *ghazals* in a collection did not arise.

It is for these reasons that I have observed no particular scheme in ordering the contents of these selected translations. No entry should be supposed to have been composed before or after any other entry. This is just like the order of the verses within a *ghazal:* the order is essentially, and almost always, arbitrary. And therein lies one of the charms of a *ghazal.* It is like an extremely dense thicket: you never know what you are going to encounter at your next step. And what is true for a single *ghazal* is truer for the whole collection. A discovery, or a surprise, is never farther than one step.

Since the verses in a *ghazal* are generally in what may be described as the stand-alone mode, I have observed a one-line gap between each verse to let the reader know where a particular verse has ended. There are, to be sure, some instances of two or more verses in a *ghazal* being connected by reason of continuity of the narrative or theme. In some *ghazals,* there may be more than one such occurrence, for instance, *ghazal* 3 in this volume. In all such cases of two or more verses being clearly connected, I have translated them more like verse paragraphs than individual verses.

The Beloved's Gender

A troublesome issue for non-native readers (and even many modern native speakers) is the gender of the beloved in the premodern *ghazal.* Conventionally, poets use the masculine gender for the beloved. I have translated the beloved's gender as female, unless the context is clearly incompatible with a female beloved, and a male beloved or God is clearly being talked about. In Urdu a convention developed in the late seventeenth century, contrary to the convention in nearly all South Asian poetry, to talk of the beloved as a male. The implications of the language of the poem are such that, by disregarding the surface differences of gender, one can often imagine the beloved to be God, or any ideal being, or a woman or a man or a boy.

The ambiguity of the atmosphere in this poetry can permit the "sacred" interpretation as often as not. Mir is rather an exception in being more than usually involved in worldly experience, but his poetry is full of Sufi themes as well. His poetry very frequently reads as what some Urdu critics have described as "earthy." That is not how I would like to characterize Mir's *ghazal,* but I must say that Mir is less occupied with matters of the "other world" than many poets of his time.

Acknowledgments

This book owes much to Sheldon Pollock's meticulous editing. He is the one editor I know who took almost as much pains on editing as I took on the translations. I will always be grateful to him.

Thanks are also due to Frances Pritchett, longtime friend and collaborator—she went over the translations at Sheldon Pollock's request, and, out of friendly interest, made good suggestions and prepared a most useful glossary.

Dedicated to the memory of
Irfan Siddiqi (1939–2004),
fellow poet, translator, loving friend
and
Naiyer Masud (1936–2017),
fellow fiction writer, lover of Urdu and Persian poetry,
dearest friend

Gradually, this dust bowl became empty of the loved ones,
Not one among those who came took the place of those
who went away.
In former times, people grieved for those who went before
Now they grieve for us, those who are left behind.
—Mirza Muhammad Sa'ib Tabrizi (1592–1676),
major poet of the Indian style of Persian poetry

NOTES

1   Also see Mir 2019 for further biographical details about Mir. Mir migrated to Lucknow in 1782 and was well received by all accounts, but he remained unhappy with the city. Many verses that he composed in Lucknow over the years reflect a clear sense of loss and loneliness and lack of appropriate patronage.

2   Mir 2019: 149. The incident can be dated to about 1756.

3   Lutf began his *Gulshan-e Hind* (originally published in 1801) at the request of East India Company official John Gilchrist; although first intended as a translation of an earlier Persian manuscript, 'Ali Ibrahim Khan's *Gulzār-i Ibrāhīm* (completed in 1783-84), Lutf also added his own new material. Thus, while the incident referenced here is not mentioned in the earlier work, it is certainly plausible that it happened after 1783 and that Lutf could have heard about it, or even had personal knowledge of it, especially given his own connections to the Company.

4   Azad 1880: 212. A substantial part of this work has been translated by Frances W. Pritchett as *Āb-e Ḥayāt: Shaping the Canon of Urdu Poetry* (2001). Also see my introduction to that volume, "Constructing a Literary Theory, a Canon, and a Theory of Poetry" (pp. 19-51).

5   See, for instance, these observations in Russell 2017: "The ghazal celebrates a love which, in the social context, could *only* [italics in the original] be illicit" (107); "Mir is often described as 'the poet of love.' Throughout his *ghazals* and other semi-autobiographical poetry, he wrote movingly of his own intense and often traumatic experiences in love" (151); "Mystics often incurred a fierce hostility from the orthodox religious establishment, for their search for God was entirely personal and gave no credence to official interpreters of Islam. So the poet's love for his God is just as illicit as that of the lover of a human beloved" (169).

6   Shefta 1843: 149.

7   Mir 2019: 129.

8   Russell and Islam 1968: 96-98.

9   Mir 1972 [c. 1752]: 23. This clearly establishes Mir in the tradition of the *sabk-e hindī*, because it was the prevalent mode of Persian poetry in India at that time.

10 See Faruqi 2001b: 81-105, from which much of the foregoing is borrowed.

11 Coleridge 1983: 168, 304. On p. 304, he designates what he calls "primary imagination" as "the living Power and the Prime Agent of all human Perception." This rather fuzzy and abstract definition distils itself into imagination as the faculty that "dissolves, diffuses, dissipates, in order to recreate." Indian-Persian poets and most Urdu poets of the eighteenth and nineteenth centuries make use of this faculty extensively.

12 Todorov 1982: 40.

13 See further Faruqi 1999, from which much of the foregoing is borrowed.

14 In death, a saint or holy person is said to be uniting with God, the True Beloved of all mystics. The anniversary of a saint's death is celebrated as an *'urs* (literally, "marriage").

Ghazals

1

Who am I, dear friends? My spirit is suffering,
my heart on fire. I spit out flames.

My own passion brought me out from behind the curtain,
for I am really one who dwells in mystery, in secret
    seclusion.

That is my radiance, and mine alone, on the shores of the
    ocean of poetry.
Thought swells in waves, with countless forms. I am the
    poet's free-flowing intellect.

Every morning I wrestle with the sun.
Like a comb I travel each night in the shade of beauty's
    hair.

Whoever sees me, if only once, becomes mad for me.
I disturb and agitate the whole world's mood.

Do not, please, do not try to make me open my lips.
I have a hundred utterances buried under my tongue, all
    drenched in blood.

I am pale in grief for the fresh greenery of this garden.
I am one of its yellowed leaves, blasted and withered.

The crush of passions in my heart makes me distracted
and restless.
Don't come after me. Understand that no one but God
knows where I am at this moment.

My existence is a mere suspicion, more imagined than
real.
Even so, I lie like a burden on your fragile mood.

I once dwelled in comfort, unpolluted and chaste.
Things happened—I have been here for some days.

2

Well, I certainly deserve tyrannical treatment, harsh and
cruel and unjust treatment.
For even though I burn all the time, I am hot in
faithfulness and fidelity.

I am adept at both sorts of love's art.
A storm when I weep, a calamity when I suffer in my heart.

I could not come to full bloom in the world's garden.
I am a withered bud spurned by the morning breeze.

My tears rival each blister on the soles of my feet,
for I have walked in your path with my eyes.

So will there ever be a way for me to find relief or repose?
I am tired of living, and angry with death.

You do make a habit of cruelty, my beloved, but don't
    shake off my hand from the hem of your skirt.
I am no more than dust by the roadside; it would take me
    less than a breath to ride away on airy wings.

Night of disunion, come now and burn me as much as you
    want.
I am burnt in heart and body, and eagerly await the day of
    retribution.

Yes, everything of mine is gone—comfort, strength, food,
    repose.
But is it not something, after all, that I have managed to
    stay alive through all this?

I'm something, somehow—that is all I know,
though I don't myself know well enough what exactly I
    am.

It's better I don't say a word because silence is better than
    speech.
So don't ask what happened. I have suffered one life and
    countless deaths.

It's only now I am able to express myself in words of fire
and energy.
And that is because I burned through a whole lifetime
from evening to dawn like a candle.

By the grace of God I slashed my breast to ribbons.
Mir, now is the time to pray, for I am hard at work on the
heart.

3

Ebb and tide in each other's embrace; tumult heaving and
rolling out from them in resonance.
So whose secret does the ocean hold, dear Lord, that it's
roaring and boiling?

The wave is someone's arched brow, the bubbles are
someone's eyes,
the pearls are someone's words, the pink oyster shells
someone's ears.

Right from the wine sellers' alley, I bade farewell to all
pilgrims.
What had I to do with circumambulating the holy Kaaba,
bound by no rules as I was, and draining the wine to
the lees?

The moonbeams would fall still, wonderstruck, like a
    bright mirror,
if you were to go out into the moonlit night wearing white.

Walking in the garden yesterday I lost my heart:
a flower seller's boy toting a basket of blooms appeared
    and then,
like springtime, he vanished.
Without him, the red scars of my heart wear mourning
    black today.[1]

Last night, opening up our closed hearts by the power of
    wine,
many of us idlers chatted in the tavern,
when suddenly a voice cried, "Remember the days gone
    by!
You men of discernment, you must also draw lessons.
The deviser of a world-reflecting wine cup—
Jamshed was his name—what is he now?
Where are his assemblies, where the wine-guzzling,
    music-laden sessions?
No sign of his cup remains except for the red poppy—
its pod now pretending to hold aloft the wine cup.
In place of wine-swilling, swaying young men, the weeping
    willow sways alone in the wind.
And the old wine seller's skull? It is now the stopper for a
    cask of wine."

Zamir composed a fine *ghazal* in this rhyme pattern, Mir,[2]
so this is enough from you. Now quiet, you chatterer!

4

My tears red as blood, like pieces of my liver, glimmering
    on my eyelashes, last night.
Sleepless I somehow saw them all through the night.

If only there came a day when she fulfilled her promise!
I spent all my nights as hope-filled nights.

She swept her long hair from her face—
and I don't know where the time went that whole night.

I wept when you weren't by my side.
I wept so much that every watch of the night seemed to
    stand still like a whole night.

Oh, the days when the power of blood coursed through my
    heart.
I would suddenly wake up and weep through two whole
    watches of the night.

You were somewhere else, absorbed in doing your hair.
And, well, it too just somehow passed, the lover's night.

News came from somewhere: the *saqi* might come!
I fainted with joy and, quite insensate, spent that whole
    night.

Dear friend, could words ever tell of the fire that burns in
    my heart?
The moment I spoke a word about it last night,
what happened was the candle shed tears
from evening till the crack of dawn.

If I wake up without you sharing my bed,
it seems impossible to get through the rest of the night.

That day of union? It was spent as if
it was one of disunion, a whole night.

Last night was the night of union, and at just one of her
    ravishing ways
I could surely die, last night.
My sleepy fortune was wide awake:
she and I met together at my house last night.
She made one of her amorous plays
as she started and woke up last night.
Were she to show her full face it would be dawn,
though there still remained one more watch of the night.
She hid her face behind her hair and asked:
"Tell me, Mir, how much is still left of the night?"

5

The head swollen with a crown's pride today
will be the site of loud lamentation tomorrow.

The peri is ashamed of her face when she is in your
presence.
The partridge can do nothing to match your walk.[3]

Did anyone ever journey safely through the quarters of the
world?
All travelers had their baggage plundered somewhere on
the highway.

Even prison could do nothing to lessen the tumults of
unbridled madness.
Now the only cure for my deranged head is to be dashed
against a block of stone.

Each wound in my heart demands from doomsday's judge[4]
justice against your unwillingness to do justice in my
lifetime.

I myself keep my gaze fixed just where I locked my eye the
first time.
It's the mirror that compulsively makes eyes at
everything.[5]

I spent a hundred springtimes ceaselessly on the wing.
I never got to see the potential of being wingless and
    featherless.

It glitters so, hung at the tip of an eyelash, that you might
    say
my teardrop is in fact a red gemstone, a liver-colored
    agate.

I went out yesterday to look at the ocean—
I found it stood in need of the wetness of someone's
    eyelashes![6]

Draw your breath gently, its workings are brittle and
    delicate.
These four quarters of the world: a glassmaker's
    workshop.

Please, go pay some heed to Mir's condition: his heart is
    on fire.
Dear friend, who can know how much life is left in the
    lamp when morning is near?

6

It's no use really, the candle's displaying its brilliance
    through the chandelier.
Not for a second does she bend her face toward it. Her
    haughtiness burns a scar on the candle.

She's here like the full moon rising:
it's brilliantly clear that the candle's glow doesn't even
begin to compete with her radiant face.
Burning wearily, it just couldn't shine to its full potential
before her in the assembly.
That's why each one of us hastened to move the candle out
from her presence.

The suttees who come to the pyre, Mir, burn slowly, their
minds fully charged with the task.
But the poor candle burned all night long uselessly,
without self-realization.

7

How I wish I were one with this garden, like the scent of
flowers,
floating with the morning breeze, enjoying for a moment
then dissipating like the wind.

I am nothing but embodied desire and that's what made
me a slave.
If I were a heart that had no desires, I would be God.

How I wish God had let me remain the little clod that I
was, because then
I would have clung to the soles of someone's feet or been a
fleeting cloud of dust on the road.

Lord, what kind of people are they that desire to be slaves?
I would feel ashamed to be God.

City of love, I don't know what realm you are from but
    really
I wish and pray that we your citizens had been created
    with no loyalty at all.

I am now such as I was made according to my fashioner's
    desire.
What would I have been had I been made as I myself
    wanted?

Mir, it's quite proper critics say whatever they want to
    say—what do they know, after all?
They would know better if they understood what it means
    to be parted from one such as she.

8

My body acquired a heart—and fire shot through my body.
The flame was such that the clothes on my body burned.

Fractiousness in this assembly results in wounds and scars.
If you can, let the vein of arrogance in your neck be burned
    away like the candle's wick.

This fire ultimately covered every particle of my being,
    like the moon waxing to fullness.
At the start, only the edges of my garment burned like the
    crescent moon.

How long should I stay here smeared with ashes like a
    yogi?
I've been sitting here so long that my haunches are
    burning.[7]

Only he can hope for some warmth from that fiery
    scintillation of beauty
who fully burns away his heart, his body, as I did.

Spending a night in the garden on the owner's sufferance
    is not worth it.
Cut through the night by burning the dried leaves and
    rubbish of the garden.

My tears dried out, the light went out from my eyes.
Lamps go out, after all, the moment their fuel is spent.

My flame-shooting sighs are really nothing new.
At times fires have been ignited that burned an entire
    forest.

Some kind of fire smolders in my breast, Mir, and if it ever
    blazed up
it would incinerate my heap of bones like so much
    kindling.

9

I know myself to be my own aim and purpose.
Do I ever believe that anyone else but I exists?[8]

My submissions, my humbleness, are all directed toward
    me alone.
This handful of dust is all I regard as worthy of prostration
    and adoration.

True reality can never gain a form or appearance except
    when I am there.
Those who see with the eye of discrimination know me
    alone as the Adored One.[9]

All praise for the wisdom of those who believe that all else
    but I myself
is worthless, of no substance, nothing.

My sole purpose in making apparent my radiance was to
    enjoy the sight of me alone.
But that's a secret known to just a handful of people.

Every bud and bloom in this park prepares for departure,
    oh God.
But as far as I know, the road of fidelity is blocked and
    barred.[10]

This injustice is extreme, and supremely hard to bear: the
    lovely ones
regard as admirable their ill disposition, their rudeness!

What can he know of the customs, concerns, and the force
    needed to keep company with those who are lost to
    their own selves?
The pious *shaikh* knows nothing but a bit of jumping up
    and down in an assembly.[11]

The beloved is actually free of charge, Mir, if she comes to
    hand in exchange for your life!
Heartache and even loss of life I regard as plain profit in
    this business.

10

What looks God gave those lovely boys!
He should have blessed the cruel young fellows with a
    little pity too.

The house of my heart was laid waste because of my eyes.
    How I wish
I had firmly shut the two doors as soon as I opened them.

My feathers were found ill-suited to flying about in this
    garden.
So like the moth I'll have them set on fire.

There they are, under the sky's canopy: myriad birds of
    heaven ... or angels?
What a space for love to keep those living beings
    confined—or are they confined at all?
I know your heart would never ever incline its face our
    way,
even if we tore our hearts out and set them before you.

My well-wishers take my dress, torn and rent in a hundred
    places, for mending.
They are clueless, these ignorant people, about the myriad
    depths and layers of things.

Like the tears that fall, never to return to the eye, I'll be
    gone once I'm gone.
You should occasionally visit and look at me and at these
    eyes wet with tears.

The eyes are glued to whichever rose they look at in this
    garden—
and that's a problem for those who have the eyes to see.

Let them now come and learn from me the protocols of
    love's madness.
My friends have long observed many other madmen in
    action.

Mir, dear sir, dying is an occasion for hesitancy and fearful
consideration.
It's a strange and unfamiliar road that confronts us, who
have never traveled before.

11

Listen to me! You found a hundred like me yet I found
none like you.
You said hundreds of cruel things to me, I brought not a
word to my lips.

I roamed the world, just one person pleased me—it was
you.
You were pleased with everyone and the one man you
couldn't like was me alone.

Well, griefs boil over like this and rage; saturated clouds
drip like tears.
But the one who let flow an ocean from his world-deluging
eyes was I alone.

Everyone boasted of their true love but none stayed the
course.
The one who deliberately severed his heart from life was I
alone.

Everybody runs after the tangible, the apparent, so why
    should I deserve such affliction?
Is it, Lord, that the one guilty of loving the idols was I
    alone?[12]

Yes, surely, there were many who dazzled like lightning
    but were done for once we spoke a word or two.
Now like a cloud, pervading all creation, it is I alone.
He became manifest in myriad hues and ways, but none
    moved from their place.
My heart had a wound from before, so I succumbed, I
    alone.

Thousands derived benefit from this garden, and yet
he who never even for a moment saw even the shade of the
    rose or cypress upon his head was I alone.[13]

Friendship is an ancient custom and sometimes we do fall
    in love with each other—
so I am to lose my head? I did give my heart away, but in
    doing so was I alone?

Whoever set eyes upon her lost his senses but all regained
    them by and by.
Yet, Mir, the one who never returned to himself till his last
    breath was I alone.

12

I learnt about the rose's cruelties, and observed the fidelity
of the bulbul too.
A handful of feathers is all that is left in the garden in place
of the bulbul.

Just observe the effect of absorption by love: in the garden
yesterday, the flower gatherer
snapped off a twig from the rose branch and the sound
that was heard was the cry of the bulbul.

Every night thorns pierce the garden's heart.
Such a tiny mouth and lips, and such wailings, oh, bulbul!

The bulbul died traveling the path of single-minded
fidelity.
Those are not veins on the rose petals, they are the claw
prints of the bulbul.

Spring is here, the garden is a profusion of roses, and yet
in every corner the bulbul's place is empty.

Beautiful people don't pay heed even to a message that
asks nothing of them.
The rose's petal-ears, after all, never caught the
benediction of the bulbul.

Your heart-rending wailings every night, Mir,
will spoil the enjoyment of the bulbul's call.

13

Well, only a fool wouldn't feel anxious after sending her a
     letter.
I myself would be mistrustful even if my courier were
     God's own messenger.

If I had a mind, I'd put my arms around you and lift you
     up.
However full your figure, you are a mere flower to me.[14]

The kohl that sharpens people's sight everywhere
is probably no more than the fine dust on the road that
     leads to the beloved.

I would go sacrifice my life for her, but what is my capacity
     and capability?
I'm almost dead—and, who knows, one only half-alive
     might not be accepted.

These days I am not of a mind to exert myself all the time.
Otherwise I can get everything I desire once I get down
     and pray to God.

The boys of Delhi made off with my heart, digested and
     absorbed it long ago.[15]
What hope could I have of ever getting back what was like
     meat and drink to them?

You get nothing because you want everything right now,
    today.
My dear, venerable Mir sahib, aren't you in a tearing
    hurry!

14

You're so impatient: can't I ever say to you "Come, let's get
    into bed and hug each other"?
Say a few words, or not; stay awhile, or not. But stop by
    sometime, just casually.

Words cannot describe the desolation that rains down on
    the lover's grave.
Even you would weep like a cloud if you should happen to
    pass by.

Mir, the world is a gambling den: what is apparent here is
    really unapparent.
Should you visit, you would lose your own self at the very
    first throw of the dice.

15

Love courses through earth and sky, love fills all four
    directions.
I am a slave and worshiper at love's doorstep. For me, love
    is God.

Apparent or unapparent, first or last, below or above all is
     love.
Light and darkness, appearance and reality, love has
     become all this by itself.

To one Gabriel appears, to another he brings the Book.
On one side, love is hidden in the hearts, on another it is
     manifest to all.

Earth, wind, water, fire: all are agreeable here.
Whatever is, is the love of the idols of beauty—what else
     can I say about what love is?

Well, Mir, it's not that I like to make riotous scenes for
     love, do I?
Forgive me if I am unable to contain myself—love is a new
     affair for me.

16

There's no way I could tell you what love is.
It's a disease of the soul, a calamitous, destructive thing.

Wherever you look there's love, nothing but love.
The whole world is packed full with love.

All praise for the modes and manners of love!
A slave somewhere, and somewhere else the Lord.

Love is the beloved, love the lover too.
That is to say, love is crazy for its own self.

Even if you proved that the worship of God is love,
no matter, love is desirable, whatever the form.

Was there ever a mortal foe so heart-trapping?
It is the enemy but also the object and purpose of our
     being.

Does anyone love the way I love,
anyone who ever loved anywhere at all?

There are no takers for it.
It's as if love were merchandise whose expiration date is
     past.

You there, dear Mir! You grow paler day by day.
Have you fallen in love with someone?

17

Love is doomsday's tumult, desire, a calamity and
     mischief; love is derangement, and a testing
     misfortune.
Love, by God, love! They should be called God hunters
     who perform the protocols of love.

Love is the orderer of all things—which is to say, love is a
    composer and master of surpassing merit.
Whatever is here from creation was composed in proper
    form by love.

Love is the unapparent of what is apparent here—in fact,
    apparent or unapparent, all is love.
Beyond the material world, love is the upper world and on
    this side: the human world is love.

It moves through the world like a sovereign; on all sides is
    the rule and power of love.
In some places love is hidden in the heart, in other places
    love is manifest.

Its tides swell to the sky, its multitudes of water generate a
    tempest, Mir.
A tumult of waves from end to end, a mighty ocean is love.

18

Love in itself is both sickness and medicine.
What can the *shaikh* know about what love is?

Were there no love, all management and control would
    disappear.
The poets speak the truth: God is love.

25

19

What can I tell you, and how, about the reality of love?
For those who know truth, love is God.

If your heart is stuck somewhere in love, well, all interest
in life is gone for you.
Death is the name that people use lovingly for love.

Sorry, no remedy, no regimen can have any effect at all.
The cure for the ache of love is love.

It drowned me in an ocean of pain, truly.
I had believed that love was a friend—and a good
swimmer.

There is no place empty of love.
It fills all space from the human heart to the seat of the
almighty.

You think Farhad the mountain cutter carved right
through the rocky ridge?
Well, actually it was love exerting its might, and just using
him as a smoke screen.

Oh, I do admire those who do the business of love!
The kinds of love, states of love that they have managed to
find are numberless.

Were there any who reached their purpose without love?
Love is what one longs for, love—the object of existence.

Well, Mir, one has no choice in the matter but to die for
  the beautiful ones.
Do not do love. Love is a bad one, a calamity in fact.

20

Quite often, my good man, people ask: tell us, what is love?
Some say it is God's own secret while others declare it is
  God.

Love's glory is always high, but its tasks and actions are
  wondrous.
It sometimes courses through the heart and the mind;
  sometimes it is different—or indifferent to all.

Loving the young softwood trees of the garden of love is
  tough business.
Love is a penalty and pain, really—if one doesn't fall
  unconscious breathing in the fragrance of that apple,
  the rounded chin.[16]

You there! Beware of love and keep away. It causes
  terrible, dire suffering.
Love is pain and grief and hardship, a bane and pest of the
  spirit—a fiend in fact.

One who loves someone contrary to his temperament,
  Mir, will drink bitter drafts.
And if one finds a lover who is not contrary? Loving then is
  a pleasure, pure enjoyment.

21

The earth, according to lovers, is cold, mere dust, but it's
  where love has its dwelling place.
And the sky? It is the dust that floats around on the
  highway of love.

The weak and wan Majnun is popular, and not only in the
  cities.
Love commands goodwill and high regard also among the
  wild dwellers in the wilderness.

How great were the people of the true path whose houses
  were given over to emptiness and waste!
In a word, the city of love has always been a wasteland.[17]

To suffer sorrows mutely makes the heart's wounds
  chronic, even cancerous, and yet
the holder of the secret of love does not open his heart to
  weeping.

Poor Mir, he wastes himself at the first stage of loving,
  though in fact he is
a wanderer far and wide in the valley of love, which preys
  on madness and hunts it down.

22

Although you never do so, yet I beg you, please look at me
  and look—
I long for you to turn toward me and look.

Love exposes me to hardship in such quantity and variety
that you too would cast an eye and look!

Perspiration on her face glows
like the dew on the rose, just look.

Each scratch on my forehead became a gash.
It's the artwork of loving fingernails—just take a look.

I longed for smiling lips.
Instead I was given eyes that weep. Do you see?

It tugs at the heart, even the color has fled.
Stay here another night, until it becomes morning, and
  see.[18]

The heart prepares to defy love.
A mere drop of blood, and such nerve, just see!

I am near to dying,
about to leave for a faraway place, if you would just reflect
a moment and look.

Mir, I too have any number of delightful graces.
I am worth a glance—if you would just consider and look.

23

Heartsick I passed through a garden yesterday.
The roses were about to say, "So, how are you?" but I
didn't even look at them.

The morning breeze woke you from slumber.
You're angry at me, but did I do it?

I walked straight into the edge of your sword.
So what could I do? I used my battered heart as shield.

Short sword in hand and eyes bloodred from drink:
you mischief maker, you cut such an elegantly forbidding
figure that I avoided facing you.

The dirt of the road trampled underfoot day and night
can't compare with my state.
What more can I say, except that that was how I lived my
life?

My sharp fingernails made short work of both my heart
    and liver.
It was indeed artistic, the way I nightly scratched at my
    breast.

Only such as I can put those lips to work the way I did.
I made my home in her eyes in no more than a twinkling or
    two of the eye.

It was like someone departing the world with unfulfilled
    longings in tow.
That was how I left the street of the person who stole my
    heart.

Well, yesterday I somehow managed to resist the cruel one
    who thirsted for my blood.
If you're a fair judge you'll see it was no mean feat of valor.

Very often, ah Mir, I remember and sing her praises:
    "What long hair! What a face!"
In fact, I've now made it my custom to repeat those words,
    night and day, like a pious man telling his beads.

24

My beloved rode out from the city and the outskirts are
    thick with dust today.
Bird and beast from the bush are hers, she'll shoot only
    sharp arrows today.

How elegant her face that blazes when she's drunk!
She drank a few cups and blossomed—springtime upon
　　that newly bloomed rose today.

The ocean of her loveliness swells and rises high in clash
　　and tumult.
Let desire's eye roam how far it may; it is hugs and kisses
　　through and through, today.
Her eyes reddening, her head dizzy,
she drank and then went to bed, and is hungover in the
　　morning, asking for more today.

You took the trouble to come calling at a fakir's home. So
　　do me a favor, and kindly sit here a while.
What do I possess but life? I offer it at your feet today.

Don't ask how much it writhed and throbbed in my side
　　until twilight yesterday.
Well, by and by, somehow, my heart became somewhat
　　stable today.

Don't miss out on this chance: bring your heart—most
　　valuable merchandise—there and nowhere else.
There's a mighty kingdom of Hindu boys ruling in
　　Hindustan today.[19]

I opened my eyes wide to see and found her just like a rose
　　branch.
She seemed absorbed in their radiant appearance, so
　　mixed up as she was in those colors and flowers today.

Love's galvanism will draw Laila's howdah where it will:
the reins of her camel are in Majnun's hands today.

She didn't take off in the morning the flower garland she
wore last night, Mir.
Was it because the rose's charm stubbornly clung to her
neck like a necklace's beads today?

25

Is it the bulbul that's in the cage, shorn of wings and
feathers? Or is it I?
Does the rose have a heart in tatters, or do I?

Does the sun rise every morning in such radiant splendor,
or do you?
Does the morning dew have eyes suffused with tears,
or do I?

Well, if I survive, I will expose the bulbul's boast.
In the dry season when the rose departs, will he embrace
death, or will I?

Look, here's your sword, here the basin to receive my
head.
Here am I—does anyone else play so lightly with his life
as I?

I am wordless while you rain down sword strokes on me.
Would anyone else in the world let such things pass other
than I?

What else can I say of my ruination in my search for her?
Did the breeze ever wander homeless so much from place
to place as I?

I promptly came to know when you were trapped
somewhere,
dear heart. Who else keeps so informed a vigil over you
as I?

I live and weep with my heart in shreds, oh Mir!
Have you ever heard of anyone else who chopped his heart
to mincemeat but I?

26

Things went the way man liked, and did you see what he
did then?
He made the sky—his eternal enemy—run around like a
lackey, measuring the length and breadth of the earth!
The sky goes round and round in his service all the time.
Night came on when day ended.
The moon, the sun, clouds, the wind
roam far and away, wander crazy for him.

How much digging, how much ploughing before
things of all kinds and hues could be produced and
    procured for him!
He was designated the most preferred of all.
God's benevolence elevated his status.
How astonishing to behold his ways—
self-indulgent, self-regarding, self-opinionated.
Among the modes of prostration for giving thanks it was
    best for him
to ceaselessly rub his forehead on the ground.
So what did he do? Did his stubborn temperament
let him bend his head even once if at all?
Oh my God, Mir! That handful of dirt, not worth a trifle—
where did it learn such arrogance, such contumacy?

27

I came like a fakir, made a beggar's call, departed.
Dear child, I offer a blessing: may you always be happy. I
    depart.[20]

Do you remember? I declared I won't live without you.
So I now redeem that vow. I depart.

Well, actually it wasn't fated that I survive.
So, having received all the treatment I could, I depart.

Such causes befell in the end
that, having no choice, and with my soul burnt to ashes, I
     depart.

God! What is that thing for which
I detach my heart from all other things, and depart?

I would at least cast a despairing eye on you
but you even veiled your face from me, and now you
     depart.

Oh, how much I longed to set foot in your street!
So now bathed in my own blood I depart.

Catching sight of you just once, a mere glimpse, caused my
     senses to reel.
You took me away from myself, and then you depart.

My forehead worn down by continual prostration—
having fulfilled my duty as a servant, I depart.

Stony idol of beauty, I adored you to the utmost,
established you as the true God in everyone's regard, and
     now I depart.

It was the way the flowers die and fall from the branch
     where they were born.
I came into this garden called the world, and now I depart.

Thank God, I didn't have to face the sorrow of my friends'
    deaths.
It was I who etched my grief upon them, and now I depart.

Bound with the chains of the worry-filled practice of
    making *ghazals,* my life passed.
And now, having raised that art to such greatness, I
    depart.

What should I say in reply, oh Mir, were someone to ask
    me,
what did you do here in this world now that you depart?

28

Just look, does it rise from the heart or from the soul?
It's something like smoke but from where does it arise?

Is it a burnt heart that lies buried in the sky?
A flame arises there at every break of dawn.

Never, never go away from the heart's quarter.
Did anyone ever leave such an excellent dwelling place?

Every time my wailing rises up
a tumultuous clamor arises in the sky.

In whatever spot her bold and seductive eye strikes
a tumult of calamities arises.

Fiery, passionate voice: shouldn't you look to your own
    house?
There's something, something like smoke, that arises from
    your house.

You think anybody ever would let him settle down again,
the one who once rose from your doorstep?

I left someone's street—ah, it was just the way
one leaves this world.

Love is a stone with a mighty heft, oh Mir!
Hoisting it will never be possible for a frail man like you.

29

If Mir keeps on wailing so loud
how can his neighbor not lose sleep?

I who shed tears so profuse now depart this world,
a weeper for whom the clouds will weep year after year.

Dear counselor, it's my avocation to weep often.[21]
How long will you keep washing away the tears from my
    face?

Stop, tears, stop! Don't you have eyes to see?
Will you go on flooding the world forever?

My heart raises a lament so poignant and powerful
that even the caravan's loud bell would lose its senses
　　　upon hearing it.[22]

Well, so be it, you can abuse my rivals as much as you like.
You'll get like for like if you do it with me.

Mir, enough. Wipe the tears from your lashes.
How long will you keep on stringing those pearls?

30

My sorrow remained as long as the breath of life remained
　　　in me.
I grieved deeply over the loss of my heart.

Your beauty, young man, drew the world's attention.
And a world of beauty remained even when the down
　　　appeared upon your face.

I wept my heart out, but my tears couldn't reach even the
　　　hem of my tunic.
The heart, a mere drop of blood, clotted on my eyelashes.

I heard that Laila's tent was black.
Perhaps they lamented in mourning for Majnun there?[23]

Friends, don't be deceived by the pious man's formal
    garment, the sort donned by the hajji.
True, he was in the Kaaba but he remained a total stranger,
    a person before whom the mysteries must veil
    themselves.

You undid your hair and revealed your face for only a
    moment,
but my heart's purposes were upended for a whole
    lifetime.

I heard vitriolic words from her lips all the time.
But the poison that dripped from her lips worked like the
    elixir of life for me.

The piece of paper on which was written the full and true
    account of my weeping
remained moist for a long, long time.

Mir, the morning of hoary old age now verges upon the
    evening.
Alas, you paid no mind and now but little of the day remains.

31

My existence is like a bubble's;
what seems to be life is rather like a mirage.

Can anyone at all express how delicate are her lips?
They're rather like the petal of a rose.[24]

Open your heart's eyes on that other world too.
What is found here is worth rather less than a dream.

I go to her door again and again
in a growing state of uncontrollable agitation.

The beauty mark between your brows
is rather like a selection dot between the two lines of a
       verse.[25]

I spoke a few words at her door, and at once she said: this
       voice
is surely like his, that home destroyer, that homeless
       fellow.

Is my heart being roasted by the fires of sorrow?
For quite some time there has been something rather like
       the scent of kebabs around here.

Just look, the cloud this time billows out
somewhat like my tear-filled eyes.

Those half-opened eyes, oh Mir,
are intoxicated themselves and they go to the head like
       wine.

32

All advice had a contrary effect, no medicine worked at all.
Do you see how the sickness in the heart finally finished
    off everything?

I wept away the days of my youth and shut my eyes to the
    world when old age came:
I slept little during the night and retired to rest at
    daybreak.

There's no question she does breathe life into the dead or
    pardon the condemned. It was just my bad luck.
She sent word of her coming, for that became the message
    for me to die.

It's not fair that we who act without freedom of choice are
    blamed for having free will.
He does what he wants or wills, while we incur infamy for
    no reason at all.[26]
All libertines, all profligates, all the *roué* types always
    prostrate themselves before you.
In my eyes you are also the prayer leader and chief in
    all things, of the rakish, the hard to please, the stiff-
    necked, the sharp-tongued.

I committed no act of disrespect even when I was wild and
    deranged.
Miles and miles I walked toward her—and yet I bowed
    down at each and every step.

The Kaaba, the direction for prayer, the forbidden zone
    around the Kaaba, the hajj garment? They could care
    less:
the dwellers of her lane said goodbye to all that, right from
    where they stood.

The *shaikh* appeared in the mosque today without his
    tunic and coat because he was in the winehouse last
    night.
In a frenzy of drunkenness, he let go of himself, gave away
    his topcoat, his cloak, his tunic, his hat.

How I wish that she'd raise the veil from her face now: it
    will mean nothing to me
if she allows all to gaze after my power to gaze is gone.

Yes, man has executive power day and night, but my
    competency in it goes only so far
as to drag the night to morning with eyes that weep, or
    turn day into night by some means or other.

This morning the breezes persuaded her somehow to visit
    the garden.
With her face she bought the rose for a servant, and by her
    stature she made the cypress her slave.

I caught her by her silver wrists, but let her go.
How stupid I was to be cheated like this by her promises
    and vows.

Imploring her all the time, as I have, has made everything
    worse.
She shows indifference to all my importunities by a factor
    of four.

A gazelle, always shying away and taking flight—how was
    she made to lose her skittish and wild ways?
Those who tamed you must have performed sorcery, or
    perhaps a miracle.

Mir's religion, his faith? Well, don't ask any more about
    those things.
Drawing a Brahman's mark on his forehead and settling
    in a Hindu temple, he forsook Islam a long, long time
    ago.[27]

33

Whoever has gazed at your face even once will live in
    perpetual wonder.
Whoever has become attached to your long hair will
    remain distracted, deranged, forever.

True, I did make her a promise to return with the first
    breath of morning—
well, if breath remains in my body too until that time.

The rich man made a house on the foundation of tyranny
but like a guest he won't stay there longer than a night or
two.

Executioner, please! Deliver just one blow and release me
from all distress and pain.
I will humbly acknowledge my debt to you until
doomsday.

Head and sword will cling to each other always in the vast
arena of love.
This battlefield won't ever be empty until the crack of
doom.

The tumult raised by my poetry will never abate.
My *divan* of poetry will abide in the world until the day of
reckoning.

It wasn't something negligible, the act of giving away his
heart, that Mir committed.
He will reproach himself for it so long as he lives.

34

Farhad should have paused and delayed before putting his
hand to the axe.
He should first have released his hand crushed under the
rock.[28]

Remember that if the fiery beautiful one ever became
    enraged for any reason
the sun wouldn't find the time even to organize his sword
    and orb.

This head of mine has been the ball in the polo field of love
from the days when you first played in the streets with soft
    balls.

The mountain cutter Farhad had no choice but to strike
    his head against the stone.
What other means were there to remove from his breast so
    heavy a rock as Khusrau?

Mir, had she hugged me even once,
the wound in my breast would not have pierced and bored
    into my chest for years.

35

The rose would turn to water with shame and stream away
    from the garden
if by any chance your face were to reveal itself from behind
    the veil.

Was such sparkling color ever seen in the rose petal? Did
    the coral ever have such style?
Just look how those lips glisten like the purest of rubies.

Like the philosopher's stone the substance and capital of
    my life are nowhere to be found,
and desire's intense profusion makes me as restless as
    quicksilver.

So powerful was the experience, my heart just couldn't
    absorb and remember it all, dear friend.
Now the pleasure of the day of union is vague in my heart
    like a forgotten dream.

The shock and fear of death crushed my powers of
    intellect, my breath, my senses.
It was as if a flood assailed my house and swept all the
    household effects away.

Fractious and rebellious, for years I avoided even the paths
    that led to a mosque,
and now my life is spent in perpetual prostration because
    my body is bent like an arch.
It was in the beginning of love that something like a wave
    would occasionally rise in my eyes.
Now if you bother to look at my eyes what you'll see is
    whirlpools.

I was drunk and lost my way and went into a mosque
    yesterday.
The poor preacher there was terrified and quit the mosque
    a hundred times—with the runs, as if from a powerful
    purgative.

Please, place your hand on Mir's chest, ask him how it is
	going with him.
The young fellow is often seen these days upset and
	restless and feeble.

36

A long unbroken sequence of broken wine cups, wine
	streaming out of glass flagons.
I was drunk; tumult and confusion and pandemonium
	reigned.

There must be some purpose here, some wisdom for the
	sky to revolve and rotate ceaselessly,
because no carriage ever went nonstop in perpetual
	motion.

When they're together one or the other is on top, or
	under, always, night and day.
Like velvet with two-sided pile are these soft-shouldered
	boys.

In such meetings and partings lives are ultimately lost.
There is no end to love, and beauty never relents.

Frail and powerless I may be but if I ever had the mind,
oh heaven, I would join you to the earth, hasp to hasp.[29]

Gone are the days when my eyes flowed like two rivers.
It has now been a long time since this double waterway
    went dry.

Often it happens that he appears right when she's washing
    her face.
Soon the sun, that impudent voyeur, will be punished so
    that he'll need to visit the toilet!

The city has now become *maidan*.
Why did such devastation sweep through here at all, in the
    past or ever?

What can I say of the scorching and burning of my heart in
    disunion?
My chest, oh Mir, has been burned as black as a griddle.

37

I died prostrate for her but the imprint of my being
    remained a burden
on her gate because the dust from my grave swirled
    around and became a source of vexation.

Having lost my heart in the season of madness, I grieve,
    but it's a pity:
I thought of it only when no clothing remained on my
    body, not a stitch.[30]

She is human, but since her long hair came undone and
    spread like a net,
she has hunted no one but the angels on her street.

Like sleep to my eyes, that restive beauty never appeared.
I looked forward to her coming all my life.

Whoever should manage to get the wine of pleasure and
    luxury just one night
would continue to crave it until doomsday.

Love for beautiful idols made it powerless, made it lose
    hold of itself,
the heart that once held authority over all God's kingdom.
The heart that throbbed and hurt day and night like a
    ripening abscess,
that constantly wounded my liver—
all my life was used up in being gentle with it, caressing it
    lovingly.
Yet it always was grieving, restless and inconsolable.
How could one describe its end, that sufferer, that target
    of tyranny and pain?
A thousand longings—and it always suppressed them
    somewhere deep inside itself.
When like an abscess it began to flow, it found its way to
    the eyes in the form of blood, and slowly leaked away.
As long as it stayed in my burning breast it endured, scars
    and all,
but the thoughtless ones took it away from me—and not a
    drop of blood remained for its memorial.

He entered her lane and departed, just disappeared
    without speaking a word.
Many times I called out to him, "Mir! Oh Mir!"—but no
    answer ever came.

38

With her flirting she has mastered the art of stealing
    hearts.
That home destroyer first made a home in the victim's
    eyes.[31]

Well, breeze, I don't care if the flowers' hues have fled
    from the garden.
Time and circumstance have shorn me of wings and
    feathers.

What benefited my temperament in the early stages of
    love—
those very medications—finally did me in.

I am shocked: people would lay down their lives for their
    home and hearth,
yet I'm told every day of someone's leaving home on a
    journey.

What do I know of gatherings of pleasure and luxury? I
    looked at the *saqi's* eyes
and traveled beyond and away from drinking parties.

Lovers of the flesh would have disappeared the moment
     love drew its sword—
it was I alone, as you'll hear, who used his breast for a
     shield.

Well, it was no mean feat that my wounded heart could
     reach your doorstep.
That poor half-dead thing displayed a blazing courage.

You may be drunk on your flirting but who in their right
     mind would gaze at you?
In fact, my joy at the news you were coming drove me out
     of my mind.

I have had my dwelling in so dreadful a forest
that Khizr, when he heard about it, gave up the very idea
     of visiting.

Wine tipplers are nothing less than conjurers and
     tricksters:
they made the *shaikh* drink wine and transformed him
     from man to ass!

The whirlwinds have struck camp; they stand around
     ready to go.
Which way is madness traveling now, one wonders.

Sweet-tongued beauty, the stammer in your speech is
     actually a miracle.
Half a word spoken by you does its work on the heart.

The sinner, oh Mir, is utterly shameless
who unfolds and displays his wet garment in front of the
    cloud of total munificence.[32]

39

It's my longing, my most powerful desire, to die holding a
    brimful wine cup
in a winehouse redolent with the wine's flowery fragrance.

There's no clank of chains now, no flocks of gazelles.
The wilderness was teeming only during my time of
    madness.

I was in the agony of death when she put my head in her
    lap and said:
"Let death be quick and easy for you, oh my sick man."

Why shouldn't Rekhta be devoid of tumult, and mood,
    and meaning?
Mir went mad, only Sauda remained—and he's drunk all
    the time.[33]

40

My heart sent a message of pain but the message didn't
    reach the garden.
My lament was unable to reach even the garden's
    enclosing wall.[34]

Like a mirror's surface eaten away by rust
I sorrowed for her but my purpose—to gaze at her—was
    never attained.[35]
The stranger's state, lonely as a footprint, arouses wonder:
he roamed far away from home but never reached his
    friend or beloved.[36]

I was brimming with grievances but in front of you
my purpose of making a complaint never attained the
    stage of speech.

No one with eyes moist enough to rain down tears and
    slake his thirst
came to him—even at his dying breath—who fell sick with
    your love.

What dismal luck: from the garden of the world
not even a withered flower reached my turban.

Beauty and concealment have never gone together.
Did anyone ever make or have a thing of beauty that didn't
    find expression?
From Joseph to the rose, from the rose to the candle,
was there ever anyone or anything that beauty didn't drag
    into the marketplace?

A thousand pities, Mir, for those who came hoping for
    martyrdom!
Their throats came nowhere near her sword.

41

He who stood firm against pain and grief is none but I.
He whose pallor was never relieved by a dash of color is
    none but I.

The one on whom you always practice injustice and
    tyranny is none but I.
And the one who even then has the delusion that you'll be
    fair is none but I.

I spoke ill of my rivals for your favor—so am I to blame?
Why should I be blamed? Come now, let it go. Is the worst
    among us none but I?

He whose lamentations you hear every night in your
    street,
heartbroken, breast-seared, it's none but I.

He who showed the world how to fashion long thorns into
    strings of pearls, and
whose soles in this desert are knotted with blisters, is none
    but I.

I have no more strength to endure your tyrannies—so
    where's the fun if you come now?
Isn't there a whole teeming world out there? Go on with
    you—is the only lover fated to suffer your cruelty none
    but I?

I was heart-stricken a whole world's worth here so I went
    away to the next.
He who was always totally lonely in your sorrow is none
    but I.

Just take a look at her style here and judge fairly:
is it she who is bad, dear friends, or is the bad fellow none
    but I?
I just said, who is the person who took my heart away?
She spoke up at once: you there, come here! It is none
    but I!
When I said, so it's you! She said,
let's see what you can do about it, fellow. Go on with you—
    it's none but I.

The moment you heard my voice, you laughed in derision
    and thought: was it really this man?
Yes, he who wept last night and told all about himself was
    none but I.

You've heard of a man called Mir who wanders homeless
    through the wide world,
all smeared with dust? Oh morning breeze, it's none but I.

His head in his hand like a begging bowl beseeching her for
    just one look, face to face.
A beggar fed up with life, oh Mir, is none but I.

42

I am my own snare in love. Love is my shadow and goes
    wherever I go.
I may be involved with you but I am actually a prisoner of
    my own state.

I swallow my bloodred tears all the time because
I have a continual thirst for my own blood.

I am the intoxicant in the world's wine barrel, yet,
like the moisture exuding onto the barrel's surface, I am
    my own exudation of shame.

My very emergence reduced me to the level of dirt.
I am trampled by my own feet like a footprint.

Existence has become a struggle for me—please resolve
    my difficulty.
True, I move and walk about, yet I am the dead weight of
    my own distress.

You imagine there's a feeble body inside my clothes.
In fact, nothing is there but a mere idea of myself.

True, my creativity has been blazing bright, almost
    overpowering,
and yes, I am a sun ... but now, one on the point of setting.

43

Not long before us much happened in this world, and yet
    some more.
Still we came heedless, perpetrated much, and yet some
    more.

My heart, my soul, my liver burned to cinders in my
    breast.
Love set fire to my home and burned down much and yet
    some more.

How can I express what I saw in you?
Blandishments of love, affected looks, enticing, puzzling
    manners, cruel flirtations ... so much and yet some
    more.

The heart was lost, the senses were lost, the power to
    endure was lost, even my steadfast courage was lost.
In sorrowing for you there was taken from me so much and
    yet some more.

Don't ask me to say what I had for you, cruel one:
hopes for kindness and generosity, affection, fidelity—so
    much and yet some more.

I am remembered with names like "the wounded," "the
    wandering," "the infamous."
A whole world said bad things about me—so much and yet
    some more.
Strange transaction, this—that you don't listen to a word
    I say.
And for you I have been made to hear so much and yet
    some more.

Unrequited desire for union, pain of disunion, my
    imaginings and thoughts focused on the beloved's
    face—
I perished but in my heart there remained so much and yet
    some more.

Desolate heart and wounded liver, distressful burden of
    grief, scar of disunion.
A pity that as I leave the world I am obliged to take with
    me so much and yet some more.

Moisture-laden eyes, heart full, liver in a hundred
    shreds—
I too had so much from love's riches and yet some more.

Why feel concerned with the times as they make and
    unmake things?
Clay and mortar in the founding of those buildings was
    made from the bodies of so many great men and yet
    some more.

My Kaaba, my direction for prayer, my master, my refuge
    and protector, my tender compassionate one—
in my restless anxiety I addressed her as all this and yet
    some more.
But what can I say about the impact my loving inscriptions
    made on her?
At each word she read she sneered much, and yet some
    more.

It's I alone that leave the world deprived and debarred
    from everything.
Otherwise the times gave to the world so much, and yet
    some more.

44

It seems to me, Mir, that the breeze is blowing all coiled
    and twisted.
Is it that spring is here? Is it that I see chains and fetters
    around me?[37]

Delhi's streets were like pages from a painter's album:
each and every face one saw was pretty as a picture.

I was extremely vain about the poignant effect of my tears,
so I saw the outcome of my endeavor when morning
    dawned.[38]

Is the rose now packing her bags to depart?
The bulbul, I find, is like a rosebud, its heart in a knot.

Friends, didn't she deliver hard blows and pain to my
     heart for nothing and for no reason?
But did you ever see any wrongdoing, any fault that I
     committed?

45

The rose in the garden seems to have borrowed something
     of your style.
It seems the scent of pride has touched the rose's mind.

Instead of oil, love pours
the bulbul's blood into the lamp of the rose.

Morning breeze, my heart can find no solace from its scar,
     though
it has all the radiant glory of the rose.[39]

Don't imagine life in this garden to be full of pleasure.
The rose's cup is empty of wine actually.

Come quickly, Mir, and enjoy the sights of this garden.
The autumn is right behind in pursuit of the rose.

46

They had the best of endings, the ones who came quickly
to their senses.
It was too late when I became aware, dear friends and
companions.

Sicknesses broke my body because of my impatient heart.
Desire stretched to such lengths that I took to my bed.

The heart—a treasure equal in value to the two worlds—
was on offer in return for just one glance. But you refused
to be a buyer.[40]

Love obliged even those who lived in seclusion in the
angels' dwellings
to come out to the market place and lose their rectitude
and reputation.[41]

Morning breeze, you should be happy you can enjoy the
garden's loveliness. I myself
hadn't made a single flight before I was captured.

Those who admired the street of that tyrannical beloved
declared me sinful because I talked of paradise.

No, I never thought God's promise to reveal himself on
the day of resurrection was fanciful.
So I don't really know what led me to think you would let
me gaze at you in the here and now.[42]

Just see how lazy and incompetent fortune is for me: I
    loved you so much and yet
my rivals were declared trustworthy while I was found
    faithless.

No one knows what crime Mir sahib committed, that he
    was adjudged
to be worthy of such preeminent cruelty.

47

When the beautiful people untie the knot of their tunics
what will the poor fellows do who've been yawning in a
    tedious wait to see them?

I worry perpetually, given your tyranny and injustice all
    the time.
For how long can my heart and brain remain loyal to me?

Dear beloveds, I have on my neck the debt owed you—my
    head.
I'll certainly repay my arrears if I live any longer.

I'm no more than a dervish after all, so give me leave to
    cast an occasional glance at you.
I'll settle in a corner, my dear, and intone benedictions
    over you.

The month of fasting is here, after all. I too, for a couple of
    days at least,
will seek out the children of the fire worshipers and go
    drink wine with them.[43]

Perhaps she'd say something to me if she noticed that I
    don't speak a word.
With that end in view I shall be silent and still from
    now on.

A whole world loves you to death—let the day of
    resurrection come.
There'll be numerous doomsdays around your street.[44]

The clouds have been light and shallow and the forest's
    expanse has withered.
I should surely now go down regularly into the jungle and
    weep.

Indeed it was my aimless meandering that led me finally to
    your street.
From now on I will accord full respect to my ignominy and
    disrespectability.

How would it be possible to give a full account of Mir in a
    single night?
A whole lifetime gone and I'd still be narrating his story to
    you.

48

What's the point of weeping for the season of youth when
    you're old?
Day is about to dawn, go and have some sleep.

Oh my God, when my eye falls on those rosy cheeks
I feel like gazing hard enough to bury my eyes in them.

Prostration in prayer should be done with purity of heart,
otherwise wasting time in such acts avails nothing.

I really wonder how the grieving manage to bathe
    themselves in their tears.
The water is so hot I wouldn't dip my finger in it!

Like the blind I never attain what I seek.
I just grope and feel and beat about the bush.

My spirit now feels much irked by its clay coat.
How long must I bear this petty basket of dirt upon my
    shoulders?

Oh Mir, were they to be smeared with the dust of that
    street
I wouldn't wash my feet, not even with the water of life.

49

It's the night of union and now it's about to pass. Won't
  you say something?
Words and connections remain though the days pass.

I am now reduced to being awarded a smile, even a word or
  two occasionally.
Well, my friend, a pretense of respectability remains—so
  not everything is lost.

Do pause a little, revolving time! Don't you see that
  my life too
is speeding away with my days?

Here I am totally ignorant of the moves in the chess game
  of day and night,
and there on life's board I face clear checkmate.

Love's relative affinities don't depend on daily visits.
One meeting can suffice for a whole lifetime.

It's not catarrh that flows down the nostrils of the chaste-
  hearted *shaikh*.
It is the involuntary discharge of the seminal fluid—he's
  losing his mettle![45]

His patchwork coat, his turban, his shawl: the drunks
    grabbed and made away with them all.
The *shaikh* lost all the garb his miracle working was based
    on.
He presents himself as a great one for doing prayers, and
    since he does the call to prayer as well,
there's a constant feud between him and the drunks trying
    to sleep it off.
He doesn't ever put a stop to his stumps.
He's near death but his legs are still afoot.
Every morning he's hell-bent on ruining the tipplers' rest,
always in ambush for some deception, for finding a chance
    to boast and glorify himself.

Mir, it's only me she constantly discriminates against.
As for the others, they always get all courtesy and
    consideration.

50

The more I got it mended, the more rips it suffered.
Finally I stopped altogether, leaving my collar alone.

My heartfelt longing to enjoy the kindness of friends from
    the garden was unfulfilled.
The shade of the cypress and the rose never touched my
    head.

I had a mind to go and make myself a small fakir's abode
    on God's throne,
but I ended up spreading my bedding right here in the
    dust.

A lifetime of anticipation, then it happened: we chanced to
    meet when no one else was present.
Fearfully, I told you a little about my condition, my
    feelings.

It's not as if I came here merely to compose Rekhta,
but I did put up something like a performance of it for a
    few short days.

I managed to get into the garden yesterday and visit with
    the birds there
and freely taste and enjoy the beauty of the rose.

It can't be without significance: my wounds seem fresher
    and brighter every evening.
Oh the sadness of it! Did I extinguish someone's lamp out
    there somewhere?

Far away from you I battered my head among rocks and
    barren lands for a time.
I refreshed everyone's memory of Qais and Farhad.

Driven by my restless and unhappy heart I finally
    embraced death,
but I gained no sleep or comfort even under the earth.

Yet another cruel blow: in the season of autumn, oh Mir,
I was obliged to fasten my heart to dry straw and thorns.

51

It was enough to keep me half-drunk for my whole life:
one little goblet of my bloodied heart.

It's only morning and my heart seems to collapse and fall
     already.
How much havoc will I have to suffer to get through the
     night?

The bud has acquired the art of opening little by little
from her half-open sleepy eyes.

She removed her veil and it was like the rising of the
     moon.
Her going about unveiled scars my heart.

There was much that I needed to do in love, Mir.
But I discharged all the tasks rather quickly.

52

The season is here: green and yet more green leaves
     shooting forth from the branches.
In the garden I saw all the plants overflowing with flowers.

How could I stretch out a covetous hand in front of
    anyone?
That hand has gone to sleep, pressed under my head like a
    pillow.

Did earth dwellers ever understand his high station?
Like the sky, I too circulate as close to him as I can.[46]

I was going to take my own life but she prevented me,
saying: Does anyone do such a deed? No! Don't do it!
    Don't!

The garden was on fire with the roses' redness, Mir.
The bulbul noticed and shouted: Stay away, sir! Stay away!

53

To let lives be consumed by death is not something devoid
    of pleasure.
Did Khizr or Jesus ever know the excellence of the taste of
    death?

What can I tell you of the honor in which I held the pomp
    and the grandeur of this world?
I regarded Solomon's ring as nothing more than a ring for
    my toes.

Is this really the way to be aloof and coquettish, my dear,
     just like the sun
showing your face in the morning and hiding it in the
     evening?

Could a devoted servant of God ever do service my way?
God knows well enough: for me you were God.

I was extremely vain about my good judgment and
     understanding.
So of course the man I thought was good and gentle
     turned out to be bad.
Holding your head high and proud like the whirlwind
     avails nothing.
Bend your neck to the task and just go on and on in this
     wilderness, like a rushing flood.

Far better if the flow of blood tears could somehow be
     made to stop.
It's not desirable to have blood running incessantly down
     the face.

It's stamped on people's hearts, it's not going be erased,
     your
coming here and revoking a lover's rights unjustly and for
     no good reason.

Was this truly the way for you to glance at me?
Well, go if you are of a mind to—but look me once in the
     eye before you go.

Invariably have I gone into the candle-bright beauty's
    assembly and left
after sustaining a new wound from her tongue.

Din of doomsday, be sure I don't stay asleep.
Wake me up too when you pass this way.[47]

Oh what a pity the owner of the pearl sold it at the price of
    a drop of water.
Joseph's being sold off so cheaply weighs heavily on me.

Our equation is like that of body and soul.
My heart and soul, did I ever regard myself as separate
    from you?

It upsets and distresses my soul, just like doomsday,
any moment I call to mind your sudden appearance at my
    door.

This has been the deal between us for many years now:
I bend my neck the moment she raises her sword.

What can you hope to accomplish, Mir, against an artful
    deceiver like her?
You did attach your heart to her, but didn't realize even
    that your heart was entangled.

54

My ceaseless fretfulness while waking has now become
    well known.
And my weeping and lamenting at the midnight hour have
    penetrated the realm beyond space.

Every scratch of my fingernails on my face looks like a
    wound.
My handicraft has now become an exhibition piece.

After the rose departed I went into the garden a hundred
    times, and
on many nights I filled numerous empty flower beds with
    water from my eyes.

Her victim's feeble and dusty body is all roiled with dust.
There is blood flowing from it like stripes—stripes not
    entirely devoid of artistic pleasure.

Not even the dust from the lovers' graves showed
    anywhere in the air.
They gave up their lives, but didn't give up their love's
    secrets.

For which of my many lifeless, unviable desires should I
    mourn now?
I had hopes from her in a hundred different ways.

People will go about in the streets saying and reciting
    these Rekhta verses.
These words of mine will long remain in people's
    memories.

Little did I know that such days would be upon me so
    soon:
now I do nothing all night but weep.

The rose spoke and talked to me in a thousand colorful
    ways,
but your lovely sweet talk didn't leave my heart.

You'll forget the times and doings of Qais and Farhad
if ever the time comes for us brokenhearted ones.

Had Mir gotten through just one more night, he'd surely
    have survived.
Farhad, after all, did hack his way through numerous hard
    nights.

55

You keep aloof, evading me and running away. It seems
    you've learnt to sprint like a gazelle.
Is it the way of those with beautiful eyes to turn from
    company in wild terror?

The portraitist has long been in confusion, his senses
    every which way.
Actually, I shouldn't have gone on and on about her long
    disheveled hair.[48]

The best an awl could do was bore a hole into a stone
to perforate the listeners' hearts—that's what lamentation
    of the afflicted can do.

Cypress on the canal bank, poppy and rose, lily of the
    valley, eglantine, buds yet to bloom:
whichever way you look there's a whole flower garden of
    my colorful creative thoughts.

The thorns became red buds after I'd gone on pilgrimage
    to the desert.
People now visit here and take away a few drops of the
    serum from my blisters as holy water.

Had remedies been prescribed soon enough, there might
    have been some benefit, Mir.
Now the poor fellows who were sick in her love have
    reached the terminal stage.

56

My heart can endure love no more, my spirit too is feeble.
So now it's like this: the journey ahead is long and it's
    farewell for me.

How joyous, how colorful were our times during union,
    and how the days passed in sharing various pleasures.
And now it's disunion and I am alone, living a life of
    alienation. That's how things are with me.

Ever since the dawn of our being was founded on the
    drawing in and letting out of a couple of breaths,
do you think I have one moment free? What and how
    much can I achieve over this brief breathing spell?

The thief, the shoplifter, the Sikh, the Maratha, the king,
    the beggar—all are out for money.
Those who have nothing are at peace—poverty too is a
    form of wealth.

She gave me leave, Mir, to put my head upon her feet.
Could I ever find the words to describe the weight of the
    gratuitous kindness I now carry on my head?

57

I heave cold sighs and burn—what splendid twists of hot
    and cold indeed!
Because of the heart in my side, I am in both fire and
    water.

I don't have the support of even the smallest of favorable
    causes.
Although in a manner of speaking I too reside in a world of
    causes.[49]

My slumbering heart—what unspeakable tyranny and
    hardship it causes for me.
The caravans are ready to depart and I am still asleep.
Those who lost their heads in love all lie motionless in
    water.
Caught in a whirlpool the moment they raised anchor—
    there was no way to free their boats.
My body pulverized and the dust settling somewhat far
    from her—that's not something far from credible.
To keep a respectful distance in this way is also in the
    rulebook of love.

Let the moon shine ever so bright, they're fully free:
your lovers, their hearts afire because of the reflection
    from your face, are always in the glow of the moon.

I too am among the useless and the ruined of this city,
    those,
oh Mir, whose homes lie directly in the path of the flood.

58

Grief and pain rise like a storm rising endlessly, my dear
young friend.
At such times something like dust seems to blow into my
face, my dear young friend.[50]

My breast is riddled with holes—I pounded it unceasingly
in sorrow for my heart.
It's not a slab of stone after all, it's my rib cage, my dear
young friend.

I, the shyest of people—and love held me up to the ridicule
of all the world.
That's the reason my eye is always downcast among the
public, my dear young friend.
Envy for her radiant face destroys the spirit.
In her company the candle stands dumb, consuming itself
to death, my dear young friend.

My sense of pride and shame triggers a fire on all sides of
the cage
when the morning breeze blows in a couple of rose petals,
my dear young friend.

Its sad and subdued lament reminds me of the song of the
Turkish guitar.
The sweet singing bird of this garden—it's actually a
young blade from Baghat, my dear young friend.

What can I say happens to me then, when my heart feels
    heavy and sluggish? My liver seems to leap up to my
    mouth,
and how agitated, how perplexed, my spirit then feels in
    the body, my dear young friend!

Her eyebrows are always curved like a sword always
    drawn,
but that curviness of those swords is their native mettle,
    my dear young friend.

How can I, Mir, clasp to my chest the breasts of that
    wanton young girl?
She ties her shawl tight around her torso and then ties up
    her breasts all over again, my dear young friend.

59

The man known in numerous cities and climes as Mir, my
    dear young friend,
is certainly worth a visit but is seldom seen, my dear young
    friend.

That peerless painter of pictures who has the whole world
    for his mirror,
oh the numerous and wondrous faces he fashions from
    behind his curtain, my dear young friend.

An evil fate led me to a gathering where the *saqi*
gives wine to all but forces poison down my throat, my
    dear young friend.

I fell in love with you and lost my heart, my faith, my life.
Well, it's truly said: as you sow so you reap, my dear young
    friend.

Beauty? Beauty is *something,* it may be I or even you, dear
    counselor.
Did anyone anywhere keep their hands off such a thing,
    my dear young friend?
The shock of this event is the mighty blast of a storm,
    when even a mountain of heavy boulders
is scattered and blown away in the air like a blade of dry
    grass, my dear young friend.[51]

Is Mir a summoner of peris, that he keeps us all awake far
    into the night?
He begins burning his heart, his liver, his soul right from
    twilight, my dear young friend.[52]

60

So you believe that Majnun is in futile pursuit of the
    howdah, my young friend?
Well, actually he's very wise, that deranged crazy man, my
    young friend.[53]

Does anyone bother even to taste sugar, my young friend?
Everyone here grants the utter sweetness of those lips and
    talks of nothing else, my young friend.

I grant the preacher is angel-pure.
What's difficult is to be human, my young friend.

Largesse from wet eyes flows all the time.
Even the flood comes to beg at this door, my young friend.

There's surely relief and comfort beyond death
but between then and now there's that deadly event, my
    young friend.

Trampling the heart under foot is not only tyranny but
    wrathful violence.
Did anyone ever pound it so? After all, it's a heart, my
    young friend.

Why dread the doomsday that must come someday.
    Tomorrow?
The night is pregnant, so let's see what it brings forth at
    dawn, my young friend.[54]

The heart is still, not even writhing or throbbing: who
    knows
what sharpshooter brought it down, my young friend?

The eye must open before the time of the prayer.
Woe unto him who slept his time away, my dear young
    friend. [55]

True, the color of colorlessness is something apart from
    all,
but it partakes of all colors, like water, my young friend.[56]

Were the sky to move just a bit away from here, I wouldn't
    be sick in the chest like a consumptive.
It is a slab of stone on my breast, my young friend.

Why such sportiveness, such attachment of the heart to
    the world?
It's just the road—or is it the destination, my dear young
    friend?

It's not worth discussing how little depth the ocean of life
    really has.
From end to end in a hundred places there's only shallows
    and dry shore, my young friend.

Look at things a brief moment with an eye that seeks the
    truth,
and you'll find that all you see is false, my young friend.

Empathy is all. There's nothing else that avails.
Medication? Well, for the lovesick it's a deadly blow, my
    young friend.

For years and years I wandered there weeping like a cloud,
and now the mud and mire in her street reach to the thigh,
  my young friend.

Ancient of days and yet so juvenile!
How barbarously intractable the sky is even though bent
  with age, my young friend.[57]

Why complain about the sad and wounded heart?
For one thing, it is sad, for another, wounded, my young
  friend.

Comfort your heart with the sight of green grass.
That's all the harvest of the world's tillage you'll have, my
  young friend.

It's the smart alecks of the world who're the talk of the
  town now.
My art is poetry—and who gives a damn for it, my young
  friend?

Yesterday, I too managed a pilgrimage to Mir.
He seemed a little indifferent and arrogant but perfect
  nevertheless, my young friend.[58]

61

Did that rosebud mouth ever show kindness with words?
We met often over the years, but she was always stingy
　　with speech.

Actually, there were causes enough for me to depart this
　　life.
I'm not dead yet simply because I worry about having to
　　get a shroud.

Yesterday I found a bulbul dead at the flower seller's.
How eager-hearted the little bird was to go back to the
　　garden!

You walked with a swagger and a sway even as a boy.
I knew from the very beginning that such deportment
　　would cause me grief.

All the birds in the cage were telling the glory of the rose,
although each and every one was drooping and about to
　　die.

The whole of the water's surface: unmoving, hard as a
　　mirror.
Is it because her body's reflection was somewhere up the
　　river?[59]

It's not that I have made a practice of composing Rekhta
    just for the fun of it.
The fact is that my beloved came from the Deccan.

The day you came out wearing a short turban twisted
    down to your forehead rakishly—
that was the fateful day, and my head throbbed in
    presentiment the moment I saw you.[60]

Like a weary stranger Mir went his way in tears.
At every step there was a complaint on his lips against the
    behavior of his fellow countrymen.

62

The things she used to do to attract me—where are they
    now?
Bow and arrow in her hands, my breast for target practice
    now.

The down is on your cheeks and you hide your face, but
    why?
In the name of God, you're no longer a boy, you're a young
    adult now.

The pity of it! Flowers bloomed here in this garden and fell
    and died right before my eyes.
A flood of spring showers flows down from my eyes now.

The jinn, the angels, the earth, the heavens, all made good
   their escape.
It's now my frail heart—and the colossal weight of love.[61]

Her sword was out in the open; there were many blessed
   with good fortune.
When I bent my neck, the cry went out, "There's amnesty
   for all who remain now!"

My pale face is proof of the grief I had hidden.
So whatever is in my heart is open on my face now.

Come and see me weeping blood just before the breath of
   dawn.
It's just like the red flourish of the dusk at evening—that's
   the picture here now.

The bulbul wailed and wailed so that he left the memory of
   his manner with all of us.
He is our tongue in the garden now.

It's years since he went away, and I miss him still.
May Mir's memory be beloved. May he be happy
   wherever he is now.

63

When the morning breeze blows that way,
something like a dreadful blast passes this way.[62]

What can I say in reproach to the mirror-faced beauty?
She freely gives her word, then goes back on it at once.

Now that she has heard I am about to depart
she does come at least for a second or two, to inquire how
    I'm doing.

Perhaps she now likes to sleep with her hair undone.
At night these days I feel confused in temper and deranged
    in mind.

Although I have left the state of the living,
I don't know when, if at all, the news will reach my people
    far away.

If she continues to dominate me and rise high in my heart
    as she does now,
the moon will lose its attraction for me in a day or two.

Very little life is now left in Mir. Don't blast him with
    harsh words.
He could die even as you open your mouth.

64

Her waist is so thin a strand of hair is no competition.
But oh heart, why think of things you can't lay hold of?

With the restlessness so severe and the love for roses so
    much so early in the season,
one doesn't know, my fellow bulbuls, what pain is in store
    for us this year.

Dear hermit, go find yourself someone to connect with.
To live alone? What's so wonderful about that?

So this is how it is in the beginning for me: weeping tears
    of blood all the time.
I don't know, dear friends, what result the act of loving
    will bring.

How many dear friends I saw trampled and crushed by the
    sky on the road.
Only then did I come to understand its meaning and the
    nature of its moves.

If only she were to undress that silver body of hers! For the
    delights of that naked body
I would sacrifice a hundred lives, to say nothing of one life
    and one fortune.

Let someone observe her as her beauty's intensity and
    warmth radiate forth—then and only then would they
    know
how one should carry oneself and what is absolute beauty
    and absolute elegance.

I, a destitute fakir, intently importuned her for a kiss from
    her lips,
calling out time and again, "Please, just one! Why hesitate
    and prevaricate?"

But then I was struck dumb when she said,
"Here, let someone go ask the holy man just what he is
    asking for!"

There are times when you're not yourself, there are times
    when you stand somewhere and wait for someone.
What exactly is happening with you these days, oh Mir?

65

No, don't go claiming you are equal to your beloved's dog.
In fact, you should feel proud and superior if you get to sit
    somewhere near it.

The time when we can be together is fast nearing its end.
    Lest you later have regrets,
you should, if you can, come visit me every day.

There's a fresh wind blowing here, worth going out to
    enjoy. Let someone go say to the *shaikh:*
Sir, should you now go to the winehouse, you'd be working
    miracles all the time.[63]

You looked in the mirror and fell still, like a picture.
Say something, don't prolong your silence. It's not good to
    be lost in speechlessness.

All right, enough, you wasted too much of your time on
    the art of poetry.
Mir, you are old and grizzled, now stop your dreamings
    and imaginings.

66

No, why be sad about my being slain? Have them take my
    body away.
I've given up my life, so come, you too should give up and
    let the matter pass.

I'd do her obeisance if she escaped with her life into the
    sanctuary of the Kaaba.
Let the doe destined for the sanctuary sustain just one
    wound from my beloved's hands.[64]

The dust of her street tugs at everyone's heart.
If one gets away unscathed, two more appear ready to die.

You never raise your eyes. You think that's what the rules
    of honor and generosity prescribe?
It's been years that I've wandered far and lonely. Let's at
    least exchange glances.

I will drink the bitter draft of sorrow; I will die one minute
   and revive the next.
Let my heart be sold off to a buyer, if it can't stay with me.

The spring is uproarious this season. Please don't put me
   in chains.
I want to let out my heart's desires to the full. Let me
   celebrate with din and clamor everywhere![65]

So what's the expanse and the volume of the whole world
   worth, once I let my ferocious madness go free?
I'll surely throw my legs around, but let me first take leave
   from what keeps me busy now.

It's no skin off my nose: I just listen and say nothing.
My heart has understood what it needed to understand.
   Let the counselor chatter on.

Mir, you're still too frail. Don't go to her street just now.
Have patience, dear fellow, let your strength be restored a
   bit more in heart and spirit.

To construct a coherent utterance is rather a tough job.
   Verse makers galore are here.
Let my friends and rivals soar high in thought and
   compose a *ghazal* like this one.

67

She long since promised to visit, but her noble presence
   has yet to arrive.
My eyes close, I'm all but gone. Just go and look, is she
   coming still?
It has been years and she says the same thing: "Get out,
   you! Why don't you go away?"
Now just look at my eager desire, my humbleness—I visit
   her place still.

Nightly she sleeps with me, naked in my arms,
but she would never look at me face-to-face during the
   day, she's full of shyness still.

My fellow students all graduated, free from the burdens of
   schooling.
I waste my time in ignorance, diverting myself with
   schoolboys still.

Flowers that bloomed in the garden in a hundred colors
   were scattered by the winds of autumn too.
And Mir, lost in his love for the springtime of love and
   madness, brands flowers upon himself still.[66]

68

Things so refulgent—do you think your hijab could ever
    hide them?
One side of your face, my dearest, is the sun; and the other,
    the moon.

In a random guess she made me the target of her arrow,
although I, long-suffering and long-drinking, was at the
    outer limit of her bowshot.
I slept the sleep of the negligent, not knowing the worth of
    those who are now gone. It was as if my eyes opened
only after those meetings and gatherings became dreams.

Nothing here but things that cause discord and dissension
    with that greedy fellow.
I have no property, am wholly destitute, but the demand
    from there is for goods and merchandise.

Has it seen its reflection in that ocean of beauty?
Is that why the whirlpool goes round and round its own
    self adoringly?

The wonder is that no one, but no one, desires it,
even though the merchandise called fidelity in love is
    extremely hard to find.

I was hoping my eyelashes would stop my tears from
    flowing out,
but was a flood tide ever arrested by straws?

Come mix with us here on the lawn, *saqi*,
and bring your flagon of wine too, you cruel dispenser.
The buds have blossomed this season in the garden in a
    cluster of color
just as close friends huddle together in camaraderie.

Is it, Mir, that someone's ruby lips have taken possession
    of your heart?
Friend, there's pure blood flowing down your face all the
    time!

69

Why should I not, as I inscribe each letter of the alphabet,
    twist and turn and torture myself like the paper I
    write my letter on?[67]
Hundreds of messengers lose their lives in bringing my
    letters to her, and not one is favored with a reply.

I looked at the rose from the gateway to the garden and
    turned back.
What use is it to mix with someone who is in no way
    suitable for company?

My ecstasy brought perdition on my head—I quit the
    Kaaba, made my home in a temple.
How could he not be spoiled whom God himself has
    spoiled and made drunk?

Lovers always favor leaving their bodies because
lover and beloved would be one if the body didn't come
    between them.

Displeasure, reprimand, the knitted brow—these actually
    are adornments for those who look like flowers.
The beloved who lacks cruel teasing and tantrums is a cold
    beloved.

Whatever I have done or said far exceeds the limits of
    computing and accounting.
On the day of reckoning, please, God, let there be no audit
    of what I said and did.

Patience and forbearance in the face of love's calamities
    are the virtues of the courageous and resolute.
May God bless him whose liver is wounded but whose
    heart is not importunate or restless.

The night I dreamt of the rose, I was able to gaze at her
    face in the morning that followed.
My sleep has now dissolved in the air; it's nothing like
    other people's sleep or dream.

Water channels in the garden seem to brim with ruby
    wine.
Oh Lord, I hope it's not plain water in those channels
    when the rose and the poppy aren't reflected in them.

Oh, that will be the day for me to go about begging drunk
    in the streets,
the day when my wooden bowl doesn't contain even a
    drop of wine.

My eyes wet with tears, Mir, are as deep as the ocean.
The tears aren't a flame that whooshes out, or a flood that
    pours out bubbling and boiling.

70

Don't bend all the time over your mirror, or pain will grip
    you from head to foot.
Don't always busy yourself with gathering your beauty's
    flowers, cruel one, or you'll grow thin and pale.[68]

You never kept faith, brought up in luxury, as you've been,
    like the rose, but
this way of living is called love: it will drive you to wander
    endlessly in the dusty wilderness.

Dust will roil and rise in your delicate temperament;
like a dust devil you too will end up roaming the desert all
    the time.

Your heart's attachments will force you to write page upon
    page by your own hand.
In the books of loneliness, you'll be alone like the pen.[69]

Not for a breath will the fire in your heart let you close
    your eyelids until morning.
You'll be just like Mir then: hot with drawing cold sighs all
    the time.

71

Oh what fire is hidden in the heart of home-destroying
    love?
A fire seems to be smoldering through my whole body.

Although the garden abounds in the joyous color red of
    rose and poppy,
everything here seems on fire in her absence.

The soles of my feet are covered with blisters,
as if live embers were buried under each and every step of
    love.

All mansions of the heart burned ceaselessly, turned to
    ash.
What a city! And how recklessly set alight by love.

The heat and cold of the times have upset the even tenor
of life.
My heart is water sometimes, at other times fire.

Why shouldn't her fiery temperament burn me all the
time?
I count for no more than a handful of straw whereas she is
both a peri and fire.

The love that fires the world can never be tainted by lust—
the fish lives by water, the salamander by fire.

Ever since the dawn of eternity, hearts have been roasted
like kebabs.
It's not just today that love's fire has been burning, my
friends.

Pieces of my heart never fell from my eyes before like live
coals.
Now it's usual—my lap, my sides packed full of fire all the
time.

Lovers' breasts, oh Lord, are always burning.
What kind of fire, Lord, did you put in their hearts?

They punish and hurt, the cold spirits of those whose souls
are burnt, oh Mir.
Fan them a bit with the hem of your garment, because the
fire in their hearts is now dead.

72

Do you think you'd have lost your heart to someone if
   you'd listened?
Had you not traveled that path, you'd never have lost
   control over yourself.[70]

How to endure the suffering to save your good name,
   which you are just about to lose?
Where are the pride, the cruel coquetry, that never let you
   bend your head?

Your sweet courtesy and good manners are clearly the
   product of love; otherwise
would you ever have spent hours mollifying someone
   upset with you for only a minute?

With your eyes kept hidden behind your lashes you steal a
   quick glance or two.
Had your eyes not been fixed on someone you would never
   have hidden them so.

All this nice behavior is—pardon my saying so—because
   your heart is caught somewhere.
Would you ever accept gratuitous kindness if your heart
   were not attached somewhere?

There was a time when you walked in pride, haughty in
    your beauty.
You're surely in love with somebody: you greet me casually
    now as you pass by.

Earlier, you wouldn't give Mir the time of the day, had he
    been more importunate than a hundred men.
All you would do was go on chewing betel and biting your
    lip in displeasure.

73

Really, I am now utterly weary and sick of it all—no more
    hostility, please.
Prey upon my life; this much friendship is quite enough.

My heart didn't feel so oppressed when the gashes were
    open.
I greatly regret having the gashes in my breast sewn up.

Did you not hear the story even of Joseph?
Now make a wolf peace with your brothers for a while.[71]

Incompatibility and harshness demand only the wild air of
    the jungle.
No one ever saw the thorny acacia grow tall and thrive in
    a city.

It's not only today I hide my blood tears from the public
    eye.
For many years have I endured the drinking of my own
    blood.[72]

Is there any scoundrel—condemn him to death!—who
    could enjoy life away from her?
From now on, it's enough for me to have been alive; I'll
    have nothing more to do with life.

Don't be out for my blood when I say something you
    consider wrong.
First just set right what I said wrong.

I suffered a lifetime of vexation and now I feel too
    oppressed to go on.
Don't you stint either—do to me all that you can.

It's goodness alone that remains.
Should you ever have a life to live, never ever do evil.

He bore griefs and hardships his whole youth long.
What's now left in that venerable old fellow Mir? Do end
    your tyrannies against him.

74

A night spent away from her gives me so much pain to
　　endure
that the next morning no one can recall what I once looked
　　like.

It's the heat of passion—what else—that makes it ardently
　　fond of me.
Otherwise your sword would never deign to embrace me.[73]

The chinks in my cage laugh out loud at me
whenever lack of peace and rest makes me weep out loud
　　in memory of my native garden.

Mir's narrative makes this clear: the candle is malignant
　　and evil-tongued.
It simply wags its tongue of flame and burns the moth.

75

There were those the heavens ground to dust before the
　　eyes of the whole world.
Yet those who scorned to draw the lesson made their
　　dwelling with those very clumps of dust.

Perhaps there was no place for them here to live out their
　　days.
Those who got up and left never came back.

Brahman boys, foreheads smeared with sandal paste:
whoever saw them in the land of Hind hitched their hearts
    to them.
What wonderfully infidel places, each of the idol houses
    here! Enamored, I
had sacred marks of sandal paste made on my forehead
    and even hung the holy thread across my shoulder![74]

How many people, of what high quality, were trampled
    into dust before you arrived.
Even then, when you came, you instantly raised your head
    in rebellious pride.

Why glare at me, dear? I won't be terrorized
by your glowering eyes, eyes I so love.

The whole time sighs are streaming forth from the mouth
    and sparks are flying.
It's clear as day, Mir, that heart and liver both are on fire
    from sorrow's workings.

76

It seems that a flower has bloomed with just her color and
    style this spring
because there's a huge noise and din everywhere in the
    garden.

She should take pity—if only she'd come for a minute, for
    the length of a breath.
But no strength even to draw breath now remains in any of
    her heartsick lovers.

The heart grants no peace to victims of love even under
    the earth.
How I wish they and their hearts weren't buried in the
    same grave.

Friends, I see nothing in common between her pert,
    audacious eyes and the gazelle's.
It's quite obvious: the difference between a sophisticated
    city-bred person and a clod-hopping oaf.

Is there anyone to tell her wounded prey, springing away
    in fright, "Just look back,
there's a rider behind in pursuit, obscured by the cloud of
    flying dust"?

I wept and a river began to flow—but friends, what's the
    surprise?
Aren't you aware of the many and varied rivers soaked up
    by my collar and my sides?

A pert glance, a wink, then looking away, movements full
    of coquetry, surprises, pride, cruelties of style.
The beloved, Mir, has many more virtues above and
    beyond her physical charms.

77

What gory havoc my fingernails wrought in anger and
    sorrow!
Each scratch on my forehead is like a wound from a sword.

How could an average human being, or anyone for that
    matter, stand his company?
He's beautiful, insolent, brazen, thieving, shallow,
    profligate, and dissolute.

Cruel one, you should have spared a casual glance for the
    one you killed,
his body cut to pieces, his corpse taken away.

The teeming city of Lucknow, ravaged and plundered, is
    now populated by owls.
In such a wasteland it's difficult for a human being to
    survive.

The days of my dear life pass in despondency and despair.
How I wish, oh Mir, I had never pinned my hopes on her.

78

People talk about the heart all the time but have you ever
    known what the heart is?
If one could look with a seeing eye, one would know the
    heart is a place of marvels worth visiting.

The flood, the height of its stormy waves, ascends from
    earth to sky:
in appearance just a drop of blood, in reality an ocean.
All of us have always heard about the wilderness, its vast
    openness and space, the breadth of its borders.
If you shut your eyes and look, you'll see the heart is a
    wide wilderness of the exact same kind.
Ask any of them, the mountain cutter, Majnun, Vamiq—
    they'll tell you at once:
in all the cities of love and madness everywhere the heart
    has a scandalous reputation.

I grieve at my headstrong heart: what high-mindedness!
    What sense of honor!
It deliberately neglects the one for whom it should
    willingly sacrifice itself.[75]

Don't ask me why I live my life frozen and withered like
    the dead.
For years and years I've repressed and crushed my heart in
    separation from her.

Mir, how much care and consideration, how much
    comfort I gave myself, grieving for my troubled heart!
Now it's turned to blood and dribbled away. Why
    shouldn't I smear myself with dust and ashes?

79

Love and madness fill the universe. The human world? No
more than a falsehood.
My weeping turns into rivers, my desolation fills every
wilderness.

In love I am a nobody, no one will cast a casual glance
at me.
If she were just to look up and glance at me, even that
would be an act of grace on her part.

Oh headstrong heart, high-minded sense of honor! The
mere sight of her would mean my life,
yet I don't look—such is the cost of love's jealous sense of
honor![76]

The color and splendor of this gathering will last a few
more breaths—that is, so long as breath remains
in me.
I am the lamp that burns till morning: my breaths though
few are of some little worth, dear friend.

The down has appeared on your face, and it's clear that
your face though disfigured is very attractive still.
Now tell me, will I still not attain my desire, or can I hold
out some hope in the present state of things?[77]

I saw pictures of Laila and Majnun painted together on the
     same page,
wonderstruck, both of them, at finding themselves in such
     a situation.[78]

He whom the omnipotent hand of God raised from the
     dust and gave human form and life to,
that slave of God, commands no price or value: this too is
     God's omnipotence.

Hopeless tears have been flowing from my eyes since
     morning, as if in farewell.
Perhaps some desire is leaving my heart today.

How alluring is the assembly of this world! Everyone you
     see departing
is forlorn, grief-stricken, utterly woebegone.

When he had something in his pocket, he spent it all on
     boys.
And now the fact that Mir wanders like a pauper is due to
     them alone.

80

Every leaf, every flower, is aware of my state.
The rose may know or maybe not, but the entire rose
     garden knows.

If the sky had the power, it would stop even the pearl in
    her ear from touching her earring.
The sky regards her as the pupil of the eyes of the sun and
    the moon.[79]

I take the name of God all the time before that arrogant
    person.
But do you think she—haughty, always busy decking
    herself out—would ever acknowledge God the
    omnipresent?

Is there a greater simpleton in the world than a lover?
He believes that losing his life in her love actually
    redounds to his profit.

There's no custom or convention in beauty's city to cure
    heartsickness.
Otherwise even a heart-snatching slip of a girl would know
    how to heal that pain.

That young fellow, a hunter's son, is so proud of his
    prowess in seducing his victim!
He believes that even the birds flying free in the air are
    actually his captives.

Affection, fidelity, pleasant speech or conduct, favors—she
    knows nothing of this.
She knows everything else: taunts and sarcasm, oblique
    comment, arcane hints, innuendo.

The lover is always dead, but regains life on seeing her.
He treats a sudden appearance by the beloved as a second
      lease on life.

What an effusion of mischief, what a load of calamity my
      loved one places on anyone
who she knows has lost his heart, energy, and strength,
      battered by love.

She turns her head away from any chinks she discerns in
      the garden wall,
convinced they'll in no time allow the gaze of hundreds of
      passersby.

Gulping down drafts of bitterness, that foolish fellow
      called Mir is thirsty for his own blood.
He believes the sharp water of her sword is the kind that
      enhances health.[80]

81

Is there ever deliverance from these afflictions?
There is love, impoverishment, disunion.

Let's see what comes to pass as time passes.
I too am about to pass, since passing is inevitable.

Bones in the bodies shiver and burn.
Love is such a fire starter.

The winking stars tug at my heart—
how unlikely a place for my eyes to find themselves
    attached.

What miraculous artistry! What invention! What marvels!
Do not be surprised. It's almighty creativity after all.

My allure doesn't reach her, and my luck is powerless to
    bring me to her.
How can I pretend she is accessible?

It's just a nice conceit to say her lips are rubies.
Everyone has concocted this fiction.

I really can't tell you how much the anger and passion of
    love irritate me at times:
fingernail scratches on my face are like wounds inflicted
    with a sword.[81]

I would never have come into the garden without her,
but the bulbul was calling out loud to me.

Were the night of union with that hostile party ever to
    arrive,
it would be quarrel, quarrel all the way from night to
    morning!

I have no job, nothing occupies me
but composing and saying *ghazal*s at all times appropriate
    or inappropriate.

Don't smash this mirror and go away,
for it's my only means of seeing your face in friendship and
love.[82]

82

That good-looking youth, that artful trickster, that most
desired beauty was rather kind to me today.
I, an old, toothless, decrepit beggar, and he gave me a
kiss.[83]

Not one teardrop now falls from my eyes.
The feverish throbbing of my heart day and night entirely
consumed my heart's blood.

He endured life patiently but was just as impatient to die.
A thousand pities that sick man didn't survive another day
or two.

Years upon years have passed with us apart, and I keep my
hand on my heart to give it support.
There was never a day when she visited and hugged me
and took my heart in her hands.

83

If they attach their hearts too much to that unfaithful
    person,
astute practitioner of cruelty, she torments them, long-
    suffering lovers, even more.

Oh how lovingly it clings to her golden body!
That sulfur-colored dress inflames and wounds my soul.

Does she intend to make me a wanderer someday soon?
Rather often of late she has taken to visiting me at night
    with her hair undone.[84]

Even if is she is fond of me, in love's commerce your value
    sinks if you visit too much.
That's why I go there only when she sends for me many
    times.

I go there infrequently but I have no power over my heart.
Because of its twisted temperament it abuses me roundly
    and often.

Anyone will forget all his eloquence and elaborate speech
    in her presence,
anyone partial to hyperbolizing like the poets and to
    making up smart phrases.

Is there a dearth of pleasure-giving and sweet-tempered
    women?
Yet it's only her coquetry and elegant style that really
    appeal to me.

She is not with me! I only hope I can sleep soundly without
    her.
My thoughts turn toward her all the time.

I am entirely helpless. She said, "Mir mustn't come
    anywhere near.
He's a bad fellow much given to riotous activity."

84

A cloud came recently from the Kaaba, black, oh so black.
Ready to get black drunk, everyone has eyes black with
    dazzlement.[85]

Ashamed by those lips, they perspire and flow away like
    water—
how delightful—sugar and candied sugar, transforming
    back into sap![86]

Majnun didn't do madness with sufficient spirit and
    resolution.
It's not my style to lose control and run away and wander.

How could we not lose our hearts to that bandit at the first
    encounter?
Her style and coquetry are shoplifters and purse
    snatchers; her glance and her wink, sneaky thieves
    and pickpockets.

Do you think love's wilderness is any less fearful than
    others?
Even a tiger's hackles would rise in fear if it entered here.

Sure, do look into the mirror—but cast a brief glance this
    way too.
The lover's wonderstruck eye glitters like a diamond.

Everything is founded and built according to intention:
    there was a massive mosque here—
when the ancient tavern keeper died, the mosque became
    his mausoleum.

I just caressed your feet and you are prepared to go to the
    extent even of shedding my blood.
What was it that I did? Commit a mortal sin?

Mir sahib was totally sucked dry by his haughty pride, his
    jealous sense of shame.
They opened his chest and found not a drop of blood
    remaining.

85

Fellows, please excuse me, I'm rather tipsy.
If you wish to give me a glass, give it empty. I'm rather
    tipsy.

Give me just a mouthful in each round.
Please don't pour me a full glass. I'm rather tipsy.

My conversation is topsy-turvy because I am dead drunk.
Now say what you like or even rebuke me. I'm rather tipsy.

Take me in your hands like a bowl of wine,
or come with me some distance wherever I go. I'm rather
    tipsy.

If my feet stumble and I am wrong-footed, there's a reason
    and I should be forgiven.
Please don't be heavy-handed with me. I'm rather tipsy.

Well, the Friday prayer at the mosque won't run away,
    will it?
I'm ready to go, but stay with me a minute. I'm rather
    tipsy.[87]

"Mir *ji*, you have a hell of a temper!"
"Well, don't be as free with me as the wineglass is. I'm
    rather tipsy."

86

My tears rage and flow: their force keeps me in water all
    the time
Like a fish I travel and go round everywhere under water.

Last night that envy of the moon was bathing in open
    water.
The waves rose intertwined with the moonlight.
Her body so elegant could be seen
like a pearl of the first water glistening under water.

In spite of my tears there was no greening for the plant of
    my longings,
although like coral it was always under water.

The wave of tears is a sword, and in fear of it
my rival hid under his shield like a turtle and dove under
    water.

Don't take the pure and chaste of heart for granted just
    because they sit low.
Take care and give full thought before you lower yourself
    under water.[88]

The fire of love killed Ravana by burning him to a cinder,
although that demon's house was none other than Lanka
    right there under water.

In the deluge of tears last night my heart was washed away
  from my breast.
How sad that I didn't even get a sign of what was
  happening under water.

Enduring hardship and gentle patience enhance your
  value, even if they mean dying:
aloewood is just a block of wood if it doesn't sink under
  water.[89]

How I wish that face of beautiful complexion would
  remain in my wet eyes!
Flowers keep fresh much longer when their stems are
  under water.

Unlike the candle, weeping doesn't douse the fire in my
  heart.
The only remedy perhaps is to bury me under water.

My heart writhing and rolling in gushing tears is nothing
  novel really.
Expert swimmers perform hundreds of tricks when they
  enter under water.

Just as flower petals float down a water channel,
my tears make pieces of my heart flow in water.

Annul and obliterate your self in his very being, just as
a drop of water is invisible in a body of water.

My tears will cease only when that pearl leaves my eyes,
　　Mir.
I wept so much that up to my middle I am under water.[90]

87

You've come to visit today, but what do I have to scatter
　　around you as love's offering,
except to draw you into my arms and kiss you long and
　　hard?

I became dust: ruined and thrown to the winds, trodden
　　underfoot, totally obliterated.
How else am I to smooth the hardships in the path of love?

A wan and pale face, tears flowing all the time—two strong
　　witnesses.
Be fair now! How can I deny to you that I am in love?

Now whenever I enter a garden my advantage is keeping
　　my mouth shut.
There's no reason I should have the rose pester me with
　　arguments when I praise your beauty.

I persist in my indifference to her because I'm bereft of
　　hope.
Should the disdainful lady give just an inch, I would bow
　　and beseech her a hundred times.

I am a mere fakir, no more than the dust. If I come and sit
    here it is merely courtesy.
Those who feel shame at these things should stay away
    from such situations.

Each and every leaf in the garden understands my state
    well.
Tell me, lovely rose, who else should I make aware of my
    destitution, shorn of leaf and branch?

Do you think I ever entertained any expectations of these
    fancy people
who gave my rival a front-row seat, and sent me out to
    wander the streets?

Really, Mir *ji* is one of those gabby types. He's a friend, but
    dare I tell him of my pain?
If he got to know even the littlest thing, he would
    expatiate on it in every gathering.

88

Mir is a river, we heard him say his poems.
God, oh my God! What a flow of the creative
    temperament!

It'll be a long time before the image leaves the desert's
    heart:

how he rushed around in the wild, raising clouds of dust
    like a whirlwind.
In disquietude of mind and derangement of thought he's
    peerless in this age.
I at least never saw his equal anywhere.
You must have seen a powerful rain shower that went on
    and on.
Well, that was how he wept his tears.
See how he spoke: it was like an enchantment.
Oh, but how his magic utterances were roiled and crushed
    into dust!
I should save it and keep it like an amulet, it was so
    pleasing to the heart, to see
his eyes on his feet and his conversation so distraught.
What humility and submissiveness were his, what
    haughtiness of beauty yours.
He made a thousand entreaties, yet you accepted not one
    of them.
Oh envy of the spring, on every leaf of every plant he
    wrote something for you.
These autumn leaves are in fact the pages on which he
    inscribed letters for you.

One night he narrated his tale of woe with such grief!
But oh, you paid no heed and dropped off to sleep.
He composed many elegies for the loving heart and
    presented them to friends.
Everyone in the city of Delhi has them to remember
    him by.

But your sword was always keen to draw itself from the
    sheath.
Was mortal enmity a just return for his love?
It suffered a blow and leaked away like a blister lanced:
his entire youth was wasted in affliction and pain.
Now he's gone, and there's nothing to do but grieve.
A pity, a thousand pities you didn't realize his worth and
    value.

89

I went today and viewed the bruised and wounded breast.
Indeed, that little flower bed produced a mighty effusion
    of spring this time.

How I wish my beloved's ocean of beauty would come into
    high tide.
I have a powerful desire to embrace and kiss her.

My heart is already captive to someone: the bulbul's call
pierced and pricked it all night long like the point of a
    thorn.

Waiting for her, my eyes were filled with dust and grit.
Let's see when, if ever, the dust rises on that road.

As far as possible I restrain myself, but what can I do?
My mouth occasionally will blurt out a word of love.

I am now an utterly penniless fakir and have nothing to do
    but walk reverently around you in self-effacement.
I possessed nothing but a life—and I gave it to you
    already.[91]

How could the beloved's haughty mind stand to see her
    victim writhing on the ground?
The hunter of my heart has a very delicate temper indeed.

She never takes a step on the path of faithfulness.
I just can't understand the way my beloved goes.

Who knows what happened with the heart on the far side
    of my tears?
Mir, can anyone have news of things from across the
    ocean?

90

She's tipsy and has no sense of what is proper and what is
    not.
Her eyes don't see anything; she knows nothing about
    anything at all.

It has been some time since I saw that face at night.
Dear astrologer, please calculate and say where the moon
    is at present.

To gain the companionship of beautiful people requires a
   measure of affluence.
My purse is empty, so how can I enjoy those beautiful
   ones?

Just like her mirror, she always displays a nice face when I
   am before her,
but the fact is, her attention is nowhere near my heart,
   dear friend.

Every part of my body turned to water and trickled
   uselessly away.
She never even asked, "Where's that fellow whose eyes
   were always wet?"

Khizr and Jesus both disappeared from the world even as
   they lived,
and is there anyone at all now to attempt a cure for this
   sickness?

It lies ravaged, laid to waste from one end to the other,
the land of love, where not a single home has anyone living
   in it.

It's just a hunger that drives me: I have a longing to get out
   of this cage!
Actually, I don't have a single airworthy feather in my
   wings.

I am now grown old and gray, and am walking away from
her street.
I don't have much time left for travel. I don't know what
will befall me.

If he doesn't go straight to the winehouse from the
mosque,
where does Mir disappear to for so many hours on Friday
eve?[92]

91

I tried wine, but drunkenness turned out to be insipid.
There's no inebriation equal to awareness.

The desire for union consumed all my life force—
and this when she hadn't been parted from me even for
one moment.

I rise every morning to pray. I pray to you and ask for
nothing but you.
I have no suit or desire but you.

My spirit falters and faints under the sky now.
This dreary and barren cage is so absolutely airless.

Everyone has now observed the tears welling in my eyes.
My love for someone is no longer a secret from anyone at
all.

Whoever looked at my face sighed from the depths of
    their heart.
Is there no treatment for this affliction called love?

How open, how friendly were those eyes before love
    supervened!
Now there's love, but the eyes are no longer intimate or
    openhearted.

Once I begin I'll go on till the crack of doom.
A lover's talk knows no end.

Time and time again I saw nothing but a face hidden
    behind a veil.
Well, it doesn't look all that pleasing, hiding the face so
    much.

You laugh as I weep. What do you know of these things,
    Mir sahib?
Perhaps your heart was never attached to someone.

92

Why weep and wail? It's not that she stormed in and killed
    only me.
She blamed us all for loving another, as she raged and
    killed.

She installed a mirror as headstone on my grave.
This was meant to say she struck me with wonder and
    killed me.

You think last night she took me for a stranger and struck
    and struck?
She studied my face to make sure that it was I, and she
    killed.

First she hugged me, then she raised the hand of tyranny
    against me.
Kill me she did, but was gracious to me first—and only
    then she killed.

You think that perfidious woman swore an oath to me
    alone?
Many are those to whom she pledged a compact of love—
    and then she killed.

What really was the need for field equipment and battle
    weapons?
With what a show of armament she killed a helpless one
    like me.
She said: Last night? Oh I was quite drunk last night, and
    then
there was that drunken fellow Mir—you think I was in my
    senses when it was him I killed?

93

Where can the brokenhearted go to tell his woe?
He's in love: his heart is not his own—nor is the heart
    taker's his own.

Far away from the beloved, the state of my heart is bad,
    just bad.
I can see my end clearly, even from a hundred miles away.

My beloved was never clear and transparent with me, not
    for a minute,
and my heart is as full of sand as an hourglass.

Every direction holds a mirror to his face.
Let's see in which direction my loving face turns.[93]

I never slept with my lips on that rose-body's lips.
My bed is this little mat made of thistle and thorn.

How can any counselor's words have any effect on me?
I've borne so much hardship that my heart has turned to
    stone.

How could I tell you of the exposure I earned in love?
In cities and towns, in every home they talk about me.

It so happened once that I untied the knots of that fresh-
    rose-body's gown.
My fingernails are still as fragrant as the petals of a rose.

I'd never let my heart be attached to you and become a
    follower of one so heartless.
But what could I do? I had no power over my heart in love.

Let anything happen, and right before my eyes, I am here
    whatever the outcome.
Like a mirror I am never going to leave my home.[94]

The ground of my beloved's street tugs powerfully at my
    heart.
It's quite certain: my blood will be spilled here on this
    earth.

Mir, I sent a letter to her, but my color takes flight in fear:
Which way will my pigeon go? Where will it come down?

94

I am sick with love, and my heart is the embodiment of
    pain.
My body, alive though I am, has the color of the dead—
    pallid and yellow.

When I lived, I never raised my head in rebellion;
    ultimately I perished and turned to dust,
and when I rose as a weak cloud of dust, I was trodden and
    trampled on the road.

95

Let my heart attach itself somewhere and see what colors
I'll display!
I'll paint my face with blood tears, I'll burn flowery scars
onto my body.

This time I depart with a solemn oath (I too have some
pride after all):
even if you come in person to placate me, I will not go
along with you.

I know all counsel and advice are an utter waste, but in
deference to the counselor
I will counsel my crazed heart some more—but will it
comprehend anything at all?

To salaam before someone becomes a prostration.
I am not going to bend my neck—even if it costs me my
head.

My head is the sole source of the extra burden in the
misery of separation from her.
I will cut it off, hold it in my palm, and go present myself
to her.

Face caked with dirt, eyes bloodshot, collar slashed to the
hem of the tunic:
I'll now make myself look precisely as her heart desires.

I suffered the loss of my heart on this road, and now I
    wander regretful, aimless,
because, oh Mir, where will I find another friend so gentle,
    a companion so kind?

96

It's no surprise if Mir knows nothing about the customs
    and practice of loving.
Perhaps you haven't heard the saying: the yogi is nobody's
    lover.[95]

Don't regard these mosque goers as builders of the house
    of faith.
They would pull down a mosque if they needed just one
    brick.
Those who've gambled away their capital are free from the
    world's sorrows.
Losing is winning in the gaming house of the universe.

The *shaikh* can use the *miswak* and comb, go a thousand
    times to the hammam,
but by our lights he's still foul and filthy, an unclean
    spirit.[96]

What use have I for special bedding, for ermine, for an
    awe-inspiring palace?
There's plenty of living space in the mound of my grave.

True lovers are shriveled, dried up like the strings of a lyre.
And the rivals? Well, they're all singing another kind of
tune.

Morning or evening, the walls and doors are orange-yellow
with twilight's glint.
Lucknow has become Pilibhit as far as this street goes.

It was I who once pontificated: it's improper to talk too
much.
So now it's I with whom my beloved is not on speaking
terms.

I encountered Mir yesterday on the riverfront.
His hair matted and twisted like lamp wicks, his liver
burning hot, he looked like an ascetic living in the
past.

97

Yesterday some friends took me into a flower garden.
I didn't find fragrance similar to hers in the rose or in the
jasmine.

The sweet tongue of the beloved slays me.
How I wish that tongue were in my mouth.

Like a whirlpool I went round and round in this ocean.
My life in my native land was spent in vertiginous
    wandering.

If I went to my grave with this charred and smoldering
    heart of mine
a blazing fire would consume my shroud.

You're what makes me live, but oh, your tight-fitting dress
    is a cruelty.
I can see that your body has the soft and delicate style of
    the soul.

I fear it might cause your body to go numb—you are much
    too delicate—
this close-fitting dress of yours that clings so tightly to
    your body.

Mir, it would be a catastrophe if she looked me full in the
    face—
she who turned a world upside down with just a wink of
    her eye.

98

This season the garden saw blooming roses in a thousand
    colors and styles,
but she wasn't there, so none appealed to me.

Why shouldn't the bulbul be proud of the bed blooming
    with roses?
How can anyone who hasn't had a breast full of red scars
    understand its mystery?[97]

How long must I lie awake and restless, far from those
    hennaed feet?
How I wish I could doze off under the rosebush in a
    garden.

When I say, "There's no remedy for me here; I would
    rather not stay in the garden any more,"
the bulbul says, "No, just a few days more, for the rose's
    sake."[98]

Come, let's go somewhere with a rosy flask in my pocket.
The breeze from the rose tugs at the hem of the heart, oh
    saqi.
The stylish and comely youth of the city bedeck their
    turbans with flowers.
And I? Instead of roses I always had brands of madness
    burnt on my temples.[99]

How can one really endure the bulbul's call? And one's
    senses are lost
when he heaves a sigh full of pain and says, "Woe is me!
    Oh rose, my rose!"

She couldn't sleep the whole night last night: her body is
    so delicate.
Who was it that spread a sheet of roses on her bed?

One should be like the garden birds—utterly absorbed in
    the beloved.
The heart submitted to her, the eyes a present in homage,
    the life a willing sacrifice for the rose.

I would never have thought of making the garden my
    home
had I known beforehand about the rose's lack of
    steadfastness in love.

Well, people do wear tight dresses, but not all that tight.
The rose is so envious of it that its own dress is ripped in a
    number of places.[100]

How can the bulbul begin to appreciate the delight of rosy
    faces and the colors of spring?
He never saw a thing in the world except the rose.

Was it the praise of her lips on the tongue of the pen, oh
    Mir,
or the bulbul holding rose petals in its beak?

99

I too am one of those the world has driven to senseless
    distraction.
I too am a fellow traveler in that caravan.

It's not just the candle whose head was taken off by a gust
    of wind.
I too am slain by my tongue.[101]

Don't discriminate between me and Majnun in love.
I too am a puny shame-causing member of that august
    house.

The garden where you are the newly bloomed rose—
well, I too am actually the bulbul in that garden.

I am not as bravehearted as Majnun, but
I too am a supporter and companion of that
    disempowered fellow.

Morning breeze, don't go on kissing anyone else's
    doorstep
when I am here, and I too have become dust of that exalted
    portal.

It's true that over many watches I nightly wander far from
    that door,
yet I at least am close to the night watchman of her
    neighborhood.

I don't understand why you treat me like a stranger.
I come from the same place you come from.

If I die, I die; if I don't, I don't.
I have obscured my face with dust anyway.

Well, it's not my way to be insolent or perverse, though
remember, young fellow, I can plow a pretty crooked
    furrow too.

I have taken piety to an extreme, Mir;
I too am a faithful adherent of that young man.

100

It seems to me it's spring again, and flowers and shrubs are
    shooting up in garden and jungle.
Something like darkness seems to sparkle from
    underneath my scar of madness.[102]

People bear malice against me, a weak and humble man,
    falsely believing I am conceited.
Well, what can I do? Such happenstance comes to pass in
    the world of men.

My existence here is utterly restless and a mere blink of
    the eye.
It's the same for me as for lightning: being and ceasing to
    be in the same moment.

A handful of poems put together with such delicate and
    subtle art!
Truly there's a vast distance between my book of poems
    and the Pleiades.[103]

I observed neither cave nor well in the intensity of my
    desire.
Longing for her I walked the path to her exactly like a
    blind man.

There was such a tumult of restless madness in my head
    that when my imagination
was ready to draw her mental portrait it first fettered its
    own legs.

Mir, I haven't suffered the pangs and hardships of
    separation, so I'm willing to submit to whatever's
    decreed.
I may be burnt or thrown into the depths of the ocean.

101

Did someone ask you, Mir, to weep uncontrollably?
Well, weep if you must but not so much that laughter
    erupts at your weeping.

You think it was ever easy to find that rarest of rare pearls?
So, you're out to search for it? Then first lose your life.

My concern is with her lips, I've got nothing to do with
    wine.
I'd give it away to a washer of the dead even if it were the
    water of life.

When I say something, she doesn't listen. If I say nothing,
    I feel stifled and suffocated.
Just don't ask, that's my story: speak and don't speak.

Your total silence is a clear indicator: you're proud and
    ill-mannered.
I give my blessings to you, so you must at least give me
    curses.

Even those who lost their hearts must have some spirit in
    their liver.
If she doesn't talk to you, then you approach and make a
    pass at her.

You lie dormant and insensate! Is this how one behaves
    when traveling?
The caravans have struck camp and you're still asleep.

What hope could one have from someone who is himself a
    vagabond?
The sky keeps rotating and running around all the time.

Whenever I look I find you pressing her legs.
Why debase yourself so? Don't let her oppress you so
    much, oh Mir.[104]

102

You murderer, we hear from your boon companions
that you mix with the lowlifes nightly and drink with
them.

Warm and free interactions with those beautiful makers of
magic are long gone now.
Now the only thing in hot embrace with me is the wounds
of separation.

How I wish that moon hadn't hugged me to sleep one
night long ago.
It has been many moons now that my breast has been on
fire.

My heart is always quivering, God knows,
because of the loved ones' knotted brows and frowning
faces.

I found the short patchwork cloaks of many of the *shaikhs*
torn apart.
It seems that sometime somewhere her fair forearms came
out from her sleeves.[105]

I was long lost in thoughts of it, and only with much
difficulty could I lay my hands on it.
Ask us, the perspicacious ones, about the delicate
slenderness of her waist.

It has a dewy freshness and the colors of the rose petal
when the beloved one's handkerchief is wet with
perspiration.

I wept out fragments of my heart and only then a whole
world came to know me.
My name spread far and wide because of those colorful
gemstones.

I am to remain lost in nothing else but the rhymes and
refrains of *ghazals*.
Mir, it's not now possible for me to be set free from these
lands.[106]

103

I cry Allah! Allah! all the time. I have been a dervish
forever.
The asset and resource I've relied on is the name of God.

I came out of my madness and became a *qalandar*.
The chain that was on my legs is now tied around my
head.[107]

Why, oh Lord, is this millstone on our backs alone?
His life is forfeit, whoever utters the words "fidelity in
love."

It's just not possible to pass one's life like a fakir without
 sewing up the eye of greed,
because the path is narrow as the eye of a needle.

The sky is full of clouds and there's a density of blooms—
 Sufi, leave your monastery!
The pleasure of the air inside the winehouse is ten times
 greater.

Because they've long been familiar with wild madmen
 like us,
the impudent city boys now greet Majnun with "Hey,
 Uncle!"

Everywhere it seems there are tigers' claws dripping with
 blood.
Go to the jungle if you can, the *palash* trees are exploding
 with blossoms.[108]

Only two interpretations are possible: the universe is a
 reflection in a mirror,
or is itself a mirror for that proud, self-displaying beauty.

You think I alone have my last breath on my lips because of
 heart sickness?
The whole world is prey to this incurable affliction.

Her deep dark hair overpowers my heart all the time.
Oh God, my God, what evil genius has taken possession
 of me?

Their sense of high honor exhausting their patience,
    they'll fight the contrary rivals unto death.
In the past as well, oh Mir, the Sayyid clan made history by
    their heroism and valor.[109]

104

Whose mosque? What winehouses? Where the *shaikhs,*
    where the young men?
All were destroyed, blind-drunk, when you rolled your
    dark eyes just once.

Yourself and her waist? Don't even think of comparing
    them!
Rose vein, don't bother—don't vainly twist and turn.[110]

Keeping the eyes shut tight is the truest act of seeing in
    this life.
A bubble can't see a thing when it opens its eye.

May you live on, oh *saqi,* with the world and our perpetual
    intoxication!
Let the wine-duck unfurl its wings, let the wine colors fly
    everywhere.[111]

Life has spice and flavor because of you, because of you
    life's salt is more pungent.
Stay a while, time of youth, stay! Old age is bounding
    forward.

Was a cowardly life, safe in the sanctuary, really worthy of
   the deer in the Kaaba?
He should have been out to be slaughtered by the sword or
   burnt over fire like a kebab.[112]

What availed my complexion, which faded? What availed
   the messenger I entrusted with my letter?
Was any reply ever brought from her but a clear,
   resounding "No"?

Woe to living this life, and oh my intoxication! Now the
   sky revolves to another phase:
the wineglass goes round upon evil times and the
   winehouse is in ruins.

I can't recognize even the letters of the alphabet without
   the aid of a blunt pen to trace them on a tablet.
I am still learning the alphabet, what account could I give
   of gnosis?[113]

Please don't tumble down from the eyelashes, my bright
   tear.
You'll lose your pearl-like high water for no gain at all.

It's nothing at all. Don't be deceived by the high waves of
   the sea of life, oh Mir.
It seems an ocean from afar but is actually a mirage.

105

Please, Lord, quickly grant some cheer and comfort to us
    pain-filled people.
Give solace to our hearts, sleep to our eyes.

It's certainly nothing for her not to write when she's
    displeased.
But what answer should I make to those who ask why she
    doesn't write?

There are roses and spring only when the eyes are red with
    intoxication.
Saqi, does springtime pass away? Wine, give me wine![114]

The sword that was always thirsty for my blood has lost its
    edge.
Oh that my beloved took pity on me and restored its sharp
    brightness.

If sorrows were few, they could be told to beloveds.
How could one give account of a pain that's beyond all
    counting?

Feebleness doesn't let the strand of sight be threaded into
    a string.
Listen, my heart: the yarn is now lifeless. Give it a few
    brilliant twists.[115]

Open the tear-drenched eyelashes on the beloved's face,
    oh Mir;
give a little bit of sun to the grass soggy from an excess of
    water.

106

Although I sifted and searched everywhere in the world,
she was not to be found—and that was what killed me
    dead.

My poetry was judged punishable on the day of judgment.
My own book of poems was struck down hard upon my
    head.

It's impossible to make good one's escape from that
    hunter.
If she didn't finish the job in the evening, she'd return next
    morning for the kill.

Last night a fiery lament hit my heart.
It was just as if someone shot an incendiary arrow.

The entire expanse of doomsday is overthrown, Mir.
The tumult I raised, the loud weeping I wept, won the
    day.[116]

107

No grief in your soul for poetic themes, no suffering in
   your heart—so what does that avail?
Your face, it may be pale as paper—what does that avail?[117]

With my life spent waiting to be brought down, I grew
   too thin, and unfit to be hunted. I became dust for
   nothing.
What purpose would it serve, then, if dust from a hunter's
   horse were now to be kicked up?

Mir, the fire in the breast is a terrible thing. It will heat
   itself into a hot westerly wind.
Even if you draw a long cold sigh from your heart—what
   does that avail?

108

My heart left me, and I earned the nickname "heart-lost."
   Let's now see what other things I become in the
   future:
melancholy, crazy, the mad Majnun, or infamous.

I stepped onto the path of love and so am always
   somewhat lost
Now let's see how it goes in the future: will I be lost
   forever, or will I reappear?

Thorns and weeds and hay knotted at each other's throats:
 rival poets. Why engage them in debate,
when a temperament such as mine is flowing like the
 ocean, rolling full of waves?

Fired with passion for a fickle beloved, I went out of my
 place, and out of my mind too.
Should the magnetic power of love do its work, we could
 come together again.

There's no direction here, oh Mir, which is empty of his
 being.
Is it not strange then that I am alone in all four directions,
 like the sound of the caravan bell?[118]

109

Day has broken; birds in the garden look into their hearts,
 and
sing in varied tunes in remembrance of that fresh-
 bloomed wild rose.

If weeping and lamenting madmen like us wander into a
 garden,
all the birds fall silent and, coming together, keep
 company with us.

Did it ever happen that the beloved opened her breast to
 me just as easily?
She opens the knots of her coat only after I have crushed
 my heart to blood.

The rain's coming down in torrents: just look how dark is
 the sky.
That is, I weep and weep to my heart's content when my
 spirit feels oppressed.

That washerman's boy—my heart tends to him quite a bit,
 but scarcely do I get to see him.
Just say, you think it's as if I'll wash him up in going to
 him?[119]

The cypress is well measured, but confronted with the line
 of verse that is the beloved's stature,
when I scan it in my heart, it always shows itself to be
 deficient in measure.[120]

The interregnum of death during this journey—do you
 know, Mir, what it is?
Tired stragglers collapsed on the road, we take a nap for a
 breath or two.

110

The scar of separation? Don't ask about it. It set my breast
on fire.
That moon never came to let me hold her close to my
breast for a moment—never, from one moon to the
next.

My heart lacerated, my liver in tatters, my eyes shedding
blood.
Was there any tyranny I didn't witness at the hands of love
in these ten days of life?[121]

It seems as if that perfect form was created by rose petals
kneaded into the clay.
Just observe the glowing color of her body when her
bodice is wet with sweat.

She wasn't all that proud, and in fact she sometimes
deferred even to me—
but only as long as she didn't look at her face in the mirror.

I hope this loss of face and reputation doesn't become well
known among the Islamis:
the *shaikh* was made to ride a donkey and go round the
whole city—in both Mecca and Medina![122]

That she's cold in her affections is obvious enough. How I
    hope my friends don't probe her heart—
I fear they might find her hot in malice toward me.
How much and how often did Mir hold back tears of blood
    in the passion of love!
So now you can judge and see if he was stinting in quaffing
    his own blood.

111

The night of separation I didn't do much wailing and
    appealing against tyranny.
That is to say: I took pity on my neighbors.

I said: How long does a rose last?
The bud heard this and smiled.

I, a tippler of wines and spirits, was by the times ultimately
ground into dust and molded into a clay stopper for a vat
    of wine.

My tears are drops of blood in my liver actually
becoming a tumult when reaching my eyelashes.

There's never a time when we find him home,
so fully has Mir gone missing.

112

I don't know what there is about the red lips of the idol-
   like beauties.
The sound of that silent fire roars through the whole
   world.

Why shouldn't the bazaar slow down and grow dull when
   Joseph makes an appearance?
That merchandise is not to be found with every dealer.

A scrap of paper with my verses on it sewed up the mouths
   of all.
It was as if the tip of my pen's tongue had magic in it.

My broken heart is not without its subtle delights.
Come and stay here a bit in this ruined house.

On the bank of the stream I hugged it and wept my heart
   out.
The cypress had a style much resembling my swaying,
   walking cypress.[123]

What deadly grievous sin did I commit in giving my heart
   away to the boys?
Why is everyone in the city, young or old, gossiping
   about it?

They can hardly be found in a newly blossomed jasmine,
   oh Mir,
the elegance and grace in the impressions left by her feet.

113

Firing multiple arrows in a single instant, she has emptied
   quiver after quiver.
Can you now imagine the state of the wounds on the
   victims' breasts?

How can my consorting with her be conducive to well-
   being? She is so mean,
I so utterly crazy, and she so careless.

The painter must surely have drawn a deep involuntary
   sigh
when he fashioned such a face as yours.

I never saw a body so well proportioned and with such
   graceful curves.
It is as if it had first been poured into a mold.

Union and separation came and went, and I was in a state
   of dismay and disarray.
Even now I don't find my disposition back to normal.

I am lowly as dust, my prayers reached nowhere near her.
She is in the seventh heaven, proud and haughty.

The sky's myriad eyes I found dazzled and blinking
when she drew her lightning-bright sword, a lightning that
    dispatches everything.

They who had their heads filled with evil and mischief just
    one day ago: they were cut down.
Yet new fellows are doing the same thing today—creating
    upheaval upon the earth.

When he was a child he had no sense whether his cap was
    at the proper angle,
but now he wears his turban always rakishly askew—now
    that he's grown to a sensible age.

If Mir had any understanding of propriety, he wouldn't do
    such a thing either,
conducting affairs with boys at a time when he's so
    decrepit.[124]

114

Well, now she seems to be in the mood for making love—
    that saucy girl with beautiful eyes.
Her skin is all moist now, like a ripe and juicy fruit.

Look me in the eyes sometimes, at least once.
Untamed deer, how long am I to be running after you?

Oh Lord, my mouth waters just looking at those lips,
how delicious they would be! Lips no one ever sucked.

The cypress came nowhere near the shadow of that peri in
the garden.
So what has it done that causes it to raise its head so
proudly?

Onlookers' eyes are spread in welcome, everywhere in
your path,
so look carefully where you step, as you walk.

In the morning, just go out for a walk, so they may open
their eyes on your face,
those flowers that have just bloomed in the garden.

Don't linger under the prayer arch and don't do
prostrations.
What use is bending before God when your own body is
bent? Is it not untimely?

The moth circling round it caught fire and burnt to ashes
last night, but the tongue-cut candle didn't say a word.[125]

It was a springtime night, I was taking a stroll in the
garden, but the bulbul saw me,
and impertinently, with a mouth wide open, it left nothing
unsaid.

The heart and the liver both are full of holes from her
     arrows,
yet in spite of such cruel treatment she stays displeased
     with me.

Everyone, Mir, has chosen what they like best from your
     poems and committed them to paper.
I too will commit some selected ones to memory.

115

A long time has passed since you put me out of your mind.
     Were you to remember me, it would be better.
How long should I suffer separation's grief? Were you to
     make me happy, it would be better.

Distance from you has finally dragged me close to death.
Were you to free this slave from the bonds of life, it would
     be better.

Whatever you do for me will surely be good for me.
Were you to be just with me, it would be better; were you
     to impose tyranny upon me, it would be better.

The wound in my heart is wide and deep, but it couldn't
     take away the body that clothes me.
Were you to invent an even more dire cruelty upon me, it
     would be better.

You never breathed a sigh as you loved, oh Mir, and
    silently you let yourself be consumed.
Were you now to paint your face in your blood and let out
    a cry for redress, it would be better.

116

If you're in the mood for the outdoors, let's go to the
    garden. They say the spring has come: flowers in
    bloom, leaves turning green, just a little rain and wind.

Color drips from the breeze like wine distilled.
Let's go forth, leave the winehouse. This is the time of
    those who drink hard and long.

The valiant on the battlefield of love have the great virtue
    of dying, too:
to sustain such disaster is something only overachievers
    can pull off.

The heart is made of nothing but scars, the liver is in
    tatters, every teardrop is a drop of blood.
That's what love for the rosy-skinned does: it leaves no
    distinction between blood and water.
I didn't wander out into the desert or the mountain range,
    out of regard for Farhad and Majnun.
In the realm of love, oh Mir, I pay the greatest regard to
    those worthy of honor.

117

In the past, too, many were afflicted by love.
Did any of those survive who were sick at heart with love?

Unveiling too is an essential part of love.
The mysteries of love are ultimately laid bare.

Numerous prisoners got their release well before me.
I couldn't earn mine, because I was guilty of love.

So you think I am alone in pining for death?
All are keen, actually, to sell their life, all those who would
    be buyers of love.

Mansur had his head taken off, but it's nothing to
    wonder at:[126]
not every head is found deserving of love.

An embodiment of unfulfilled desire: that's how everyone
    leaves this world
with whom love was much in love.

There has never been a head offered for sale after mine, to
    this day.
For ages now there has been a slump in the market of love.

Should your heart be entangled somewhere, keep it
    hidden in your soul.
There is no benefit or good omen in giving voice to your
    love.

Liberated by death, he found himself in the fetters of
    language.
In short, did the prisoner of love ever find release?[127]

It's hard to live the life under the sword,
however strong a desire our friends may have in their
    heads for love.
In this land we've seen even the Rustams of the world with
    their pretensions cut down
when they sustained a full blow from love.[128]

That newcomer, that novice ultimately lost his life.
How I wish Mir hadn't been so keen on love.

118

Sensual fool, you falsely harbor thoughts of comfort in
    love.
In this land the currency is pain and scar and sorrow and
    hardship.

The earth is much like a painting of the unconscious or the
    stupefied.
The state of things in this gathering hasn't been too good
    ever since it was assembled.

The world overflows with the effulgent appearance of the
    beloved.
Develop the power of sight first, then enjoy the spectacle
    of its maker's power.

Majnun's soul has departed, yet it still wanders in search
    of Laila.
Whomever love ensnares, even death cannot release.

Calm endurance is an ally, but fainthearted. Otherwise our
    meeting last night
would have seen both her hauteur and my submissiveness
    yield to one bold move.

To cast a despairing eye on the hunter is more than
    abundant good fortune.
Oh mortally wounded prey, the window of the leisure to
    look is very narrow.
The heart is so ravaged, it's impossible to know
if there was ever any habitation here or if it has been a
    wilderness for a long, long time.

Her drunken eye caused the entire house of piety to be laid
    waste.
It's a long time since the whole business of dutifulness,
    obedience, abstinence was shut down.

Tread carefully, oh Mir, or its tip will push up through
    your heart,
for sharper than her eyelashes is the thorn of love's
    wilderness.

119

My cold sighs in the morning doused the fire in my heart.
That was some breeze, it put me out like a lamp.

The morning breeze was so foolish: unaware of the danger,
    it made her rise from bed.
For nothing it awoke that mischief of the age.

My love had remained secret so far, and today
the faintness of my heart forced the curtain up.

In this world where the surf swells all the time, what a pity
    the fates
erased me like a bubble of water.

Her sword was my adversary. So finally, love
organized a combat and made us hug each other.

They all passed on, the tumult of "we" and "I" in their
    heads.
That fiction ultimately put them all to sleep.

When I asked, is there any sign of those whom love made
    wanderers in the wilderness?
The breeze took a handful of dust and scattered it.

All the organs in my body streamed away like water.
The melting power of love made my life flow away.

There was nothing not in the treasury of eternity when
    time began, but my stars just weren't right.
A broken heart was all that the fates made my portion.

It's as if I alone had to settle love's account,
a thing of such value as my heart: and I invested it there.

It will long remain in my memory, that mere glimpse of
    your face
that erased from my heart the radiance of the moon.

Simpleton that I was, I surrendered my life:
I gave her my heart but that wasn't all, I gave my head too.

I can smell something like a burnt kebab.
It seems that the fire of sorrow has burned away my liver
    as well.

It did no good when my friends made me tell of the ache in
    my heart.
The pain of my story brought tears to everyone's eyes.

She merely drew her sword, Mir, but the daring of my love
made a spectacular show for a glorious moment.

120

There was a time when Mir—before tyranny killed him—
    was young.
His style of poetry aroused tumult and lamentation.
The page on which his poetry was inscribed was a packet
    of magic.
He recited his *ghazal* and people raptly gazed at his face. A
    strange and wondrous sight it was.
In Delhi, on whichever street he would wander, with
    afflicted heart,
there walked with him a noise and turmoil like doomsday.
He wasn't ever downcast, like dust sodden with water:
he was a storm, a terrible wonderful thing; a clamor that
    shook the whole world.

The desire to get just a glimpse of the beloved—how keen
    it was!—was buried with me,
even the flowers growing on my grave seemed to be
    looking anxiously around.

Majnun trying to compete with me in madness—how
    futile!
Where was he at the time I went mad?

I was unmindful of the state of my wounded heart.
That treasure was hidden in this very body, this treasure-
    store of wrack and ruin.

How strong was Farhad in hewing away at the rocks,
friendless though he was, powerless, exhausted.

Was anyone in the world, Mir, ignorant of you?
And yet when you ceased to be, no name or trace of you
    was to be found.

121

She pulled the hem of her dress from my hands.
Now what can I do besides tear my collar into shreds?

She who, time out of mind, gave me life through her lips,
that loving lady has now become my mortal enemy.

I remember those moments of togetherness, those
    moments of intimacy
when, as she changed her dress, she made me wear her
    jewels and her makeup in fun.

What has happened to that oneness? She was once by my
    side,
and now, strange to see, she veils her face before me.

The way a weeping willow's branches seem disarrayed:
that was how, in my madness at one time, my hair used to
    flow every which way.

A hundred problems face me in love.
I don't know how, if at all, things can become easy for me.

There's no one, Mir, who isn't pleased with the fakir's
    state,
just see how happy my barren, desolate house seems to be!

122

It was nothing of my doing, nor the doing even of that
    inventor of cruelties.
It was open, blatant tyranny perpetrated with the aid and
    abetment of love.

Was Shirin's beauty such that those with wounded hearts
    should die for it?
Whatever happened, it happened because Farhad wanted
    it to be.

It's only the sweet-singing birds that are captured, Mir.
This cruelty was done to me because of my lamentations
    in the morning.

123

Love has earned ill fame through the world, causing
    reputations to be lost,
but my problem is my heart inclines to that proud
    creature, the wealth and substance of God's world.

The moon, though a mirror, bears black spots that are
    nothing but this:
jealousy-scars from the grief caused by her fair face.

She was there when my soul left my body, but her eye
    never fell upon me.
I depart this world, scarred by my beloved's indifference.

Despite great efforts, I couldn't go and abase myself at
    anyone's door.
Each hair of my body is a tongue giving thanks for my
    broken legs.

Then it was the breeze that absorbed her radiant color and
    bloodied my heart,
and now it's my liver, totally withered and faded because
    of the dark red of her henna.

I hear she might visit me, and I am destitute. So I have
    decided to hand over my life to her.
What can I say? How great was my anxiety about what to
    give her as an offering when she revealed her face!

Each limb of his body, Mir, is in severe constant pain like a
    dislocated limb:
whoever is a tyrannized victim of the pain of her
    separation.

124

Remember the words I utter—you won't hear such ever
    again.
And if you hear someone read from them you'll remain
    overwhelmed with the passions of pain and pleasure
    for a long, long time.
You'll make much effort and search to find how to write in
    this style of mine.
You'll cultivate the company of the erudite, the
    accomplished, and read with them and try to acquire
    skills that were mine.
And when your heart won't find solace in exchanging
    words and ideas with friends,

the fire of grief will blow in your body and you'll burn and
    roast in it.
Mir's poems are so charged with emotion's fire they will
    fill your inner self to the brim with burns and bruises.
Pale and wan you'll wander the city, collecting fresh scars
    all along the way.

NOTES

1   It was a convention—used by Mir frequently—to write a verse or two in praise of a craftsman's or a professional's young boy: boys, for instance, of a wine seller, a flower seller, a builder, a goldsmith, and so on. Sometimes the tone is ironical or self-mocking; at other times the tone is less ambiguous and the meaning tilts toward homosexuality or boy love.

2   Zamir was the pen-name of several Persian and Urdu poets; it is not clear which one might be referred to in this verse.

3   The partridge, or mountain quail, is supposed to have a swaggering, drunken, and most attractive walk.

4   "Doomsday" is the Islamic judgment day, when the dead will arise and be held accountable for their sins; by extension, it's used for any terrible disaster or calamity.

5   The mirror reflects everything that comes before it, but the lover's eye always reflects the beloved.

6   The lover weeping copious tears is a common trope. Mir has used the theme with great variety, adding occasionally an effect of levity combined with satire (on the ocean), and gravity (because it is the lover's fate to weep always) as here.

7   In India, people often sit on the floor (carpeted or not) or on the ground. They sit cross-legged, or with their legs tucked under their thighs.

8   This verse and the next four express a state of supreme spiritual elevation, when the Sufi finds himself completely immersed in God. It is a state that some Sufi orders describe as *sair fi'allāh* (Arabic, "traveling into God").

9   "Adored One": *maʿbūd,* "one who is worshiped." Theologically, the One and Only God is Maʿbūd. In everyday Urdu, it means "the one whom one worships." It does not necessarily mean God.

10 This verse is a comment on the state of man in the universe: love is not requited, the lover is fated to be alone. Fidelity does not exist. The rose, once gone, never returns. The poet expresses regret and surprise that every bud and bloom is preparing to depart, and leaves us with an ambiguity: where are they going? The road of fidelity is blocked as far as he knows. Return is not possible.

11 That is, doing the ritual Muslim prayer (*namāz*), which involves repeated bending, prostrating, and rising.

12 The beloved is conventionally imagined as unresponsive, unhearing, cold; hence the beloveds are also cruel. Since the idols also are ideally beautiful and unresponsive and unhearing, the beloved is sometimes described as a *but,* or idol. Since loving and worshiping are practically the same, the lover is conceived as an idol-worshiper, and, therefore, infidel.

13 Because of its straightness and because it is neither tall nor short, and it is evergreen, the *sarv* is the most widely used trope in Persian and Urdu for the beloved's stature. "Cypress" is the best available translation, though not ideal.

14 The person addressed here is a female, the verse testifying to the admiration, widely shared, for the plus-sized woman.

15 Mir thought of Delhi as his own home city; the way he spelled it made it resemble an adjective meaning "pertaining to the heart."

16 The apple is a common trope for the beloved's chin.

17 "True path": *dīn.* The word more often means "religion," i.e., Islam. My translation maintains the required suggestion of generality.

18 It is apparently the lover's face whose color has faded in disunion. But there are other possibilities, which I have tried to preserve through ambiguity: (1) The lover will make such torrid, stormy love through the night that his color will fade (due to exertion); (2) the beloved's color will fade because of the same exhausting, stormy participation in the lovemaking; (3) the flowers that were fresh last night but have now wilted overnight; (4) it is the color of the night that fades as morning arrives; in other words, the dawn is especially beautiful here at my dwelling.

19 "Hindu" means "Indian."

20 The text is *sadā kar chale,* "called and went away," but *sadā karnā* has also a special meaning: "for the beggar to use the special intonation and words used for begging."

21 In the *ghazal* world, the counselor is the stock figure of the man of worldly prudence and efficiency; he is always scolding and cajoling the lover, vainly urging him to change his self-destructive ways.

22 The caravan bell is lonely and melancholy because the bell moves on with the caravan but its sound remains behind (a frequent theme in Mir).

23 Black is the color of mourning. Most Arabian tents were black anyway because they were made of felt or leather. But the speaker

here implies that Laila's tent was black because they mourned for Majnun in it.

24 The point here is that the rose petal seems bluish when crushed. So do her lips when crushed with kisses.

25 *Ghazals* in Urdu are written generally with two lines of a verse opposite each other in the same line. The reader customarily put a dot between the two lines of a verse to indicate approval, sometimes with the view of compiling a selection.

26 Mir makes a rather petulant statement about free will and predestination, but he escapes censure by pretending that he is talking about the human beloved.

27 "Islam" here represents hypocrisy and surface homage to the Truth. Marking one's forehead with the sign of a Brahman and taking a seat in the Hindu temple denotes rejection of the conventional, hypocritical observance of religion.

28 "For the hand to be under a rock" is a phrase translated from the Persian and quite popular in Urdu to signify an insoluble difficulty or problem, something inherent in the situation and not created by the protagonist.

29 The earth is supposed to be a box, or a container; the sky, its lid, is attached with hasps or hinges.

30 Nothing remained to bandage the wounded heart, because in madness he had already ripped away all his clothes.

31 Thieves would often hire a suitable lodging near the house they intended to burgle, thus giving themselves time to reconnoiter. Mir's verse has the additional beauty of "making a home in the eyes," an idiom meaning to become someone's sweetheart.

32 A wet hem signifies sinfulness. The point is that God in his infinite mercy and munificence will forgive all sinners. The cloud is the symbol of God's munificence because (1) rain brings fertility and growth; (2) God's bounty is free for all, like the rain; and (3) God will forgive the sinners, that is, those whose garments are wet. Now to display one's sinfulness in front of God's bountiful cloud ready to rain wetness all over the place is shamelessness because the wet garment will be made all the wetter by the cloud, washing away the sin. Thus the garment would still be wet, but not with sin. It would be a truly shameless person who should boast of his sinfulness in front of the cloud of total mercy.

33 "Tumult," *shorish,* suggests also the sense of enjoyment caused by the passionate tone of the poem; "mood," *kaifiyat,* also has the

sense of "the effect of wine," thus "subtle enjoyment"; "meaning," *ma'ni,* also has the sense of theme of a poem, or verse. The reference here to Sauda (Mir's most prominent contemporary) as *mastana* (dead drunk, surely conventional) is to a verse by Sauda himself in a two-verse *ghazal* in the rhyme and meter of Mir's *ghazal* translated here. The second verse of that *ghazal* by Sauda is *binā hī uth gayī yāro ghazal ke khūb kahne kī / gayā Mazmūn duniyā se rahā Saudā so mastāna* (Friends, the very foundation for composing *ghazals* well is now gone from the world / Mazmun has left this world and Sauda is always drunk) (Sauda 2001: 343). Mazmun died in 1744/1745. There is a pun here because *mazmun* means "theme," specifically "a theme or themes used in poetry.

34   The speaker here is a bird in a cage (symbolizing a lover caught in love's snare).

35   The mirror in classical Urdu and Persian poetry is typically made of some metal, generally steel, copper, or bronze. The mirror in the text grieves because its function to reflect figures and faces was not fulfilled. In effect, it is the mirror that gazes at a person looking into it. Here the mirror is grieving because the beloved never came before it.

36   A single footprint is the symbol of wonder and loneliness because, though created by a moving person, it does not move and has no companion. Stasis indicates wonder.

37   Any natural wind is conventionally seen as intertwined waves or moving, undulating coils. From here it is not far to imagine the breeze as a cluster of chains. The assumption (not unknown in the Western world too) was that madness, especially the lovers' madness, reappeared or intensified in spring, and the commonest treatment for intensely deranged persons was for them to be put in chains.

38   That is, nothing happened, the dawn was as rosy as ever and the tears had not even reached the beloved's doorstep.

39   On account of its redness, the scar is often seen as a lamp, or a rose.

40   "Two worlds": the human and the eternal.

41   Two angels boasted of their imperviousness to temptation. God sent them down into the world where they fell in love with a dancing girl called Zuhra. They were punished with being hung upside down in a well, and the dancing girl became the planet Venus.

42   Some Qur'anic verses suggest that God will let himself be physically observed by human beings on the day of resurrection.

43   Open drinking is not allowed to the Muslims in the month of Ramadan. The point here is that he will enjoy both the drinking and the company of goodlooking young people from the fire worshipers' families. There was no prohibition on public drinking among the fire worshipers. (Fire worshipers, almost always Iranian, were regarded as goodlooking.) Lastly, he will enjoy being irreverent.

44   The convention is that those who die for love of the beloved are buried around her city, or street.

45   The word in the text is *dhat,* which means "metal" and also "semen." It was believed by medieval medicine that venereal disease or sexual weakness could cause the patient to often ejaculate involuntarily and even without tumescence, or while passing urine. The condition was called *jiryān-e manī,* the actual term used in the text. There is no true translation of it in English, though *gonorrhoea simplex* comes close enough.

46   This verse is in praise of Ali, the Prophet's son-in-law and the first Shi'a imam according to the Shi'a doctrine. He was the fourth caliph of Islam and is revered greatly all over the Islamic world.

47   "This way," the beloved's street. Lovers, slain by the beloved or by love, prefer to be buried in or near the beloved's home and allowed to lie undisturbed. The convention is that love's martyr, having lived a life of torment, sleeps a very deep sleep. But he does need to be awake when God assembles the final court on doomsday so that he may seek justice from God for the inequities that he suffered at the hands of his beloved. (Also, he would love to see her again.)

48   Almost all portraits of high-born women, especially women of the nobility, were imaginary, based on a description of the subject, not a visual observation.

49   Muslim philosophy teaches that things happen in the world because God causes them to happen. He is the causer of all causes but often he does not act directly; he uses man to bring about the desired result, and man can act only through some cause (or means) provided to him by God. That's why the world is often described as *'ālam-e asbāb* (the world of causes).

50   Given the range of meanings of *miyān,* no single satisfactory or even approximate translation can be found. In the interest of consistency, I translate it as "my dear young friend" wherever it

appears as the refrain in this *ghazal* and *ghazal* 59; in *ghazal* 60 I translate it as "my dear friend." I have made other choices in other *ghazals*, according to context.

51 The "event" is suddenly falling in love. A little remotely, it might also signify the state of being away from the beloved.

52 In some occult practices, one could summon a peri or a jinn by reciting certain words of power and burning specified incense. The process was performed nonstop through the night and could need repetition until the objective was attained.

53 The howdah in which Laila travels, riding her camel.

54 A Persian proverb, *shab hāmil ast tā fardā che zayad,* translated almost literally here by the poet. It was not an uncommon practice until about the mid-nineteenth century to literally translate a Persian phrase or proverb into Urdu.

55 The "prayer" could refer to the early morning prayer or the funeral prayer. A marvelous example of how wordplay can enhance the meaning of a verse.

56 Some Sufis have described the various stages of the soul's journey to truth in terms of colors: each stage has a color of its own, but the ultimate stage has *al-launu lā launa lahu* (Arabic), a color that has no color at all.

57 The sky is regarded as ancient because it seems to be bending earthward, like an old woman's back, from wherever one may look. Reviled for its cruelty, heartlessness, and wayward ways, the sky is a convenient topos for referring to destiny, or God, or the omnipotent will.

58 "Perfect" could mean a perfect man, in the Sufi sense: *insān-e kāmil* ("the man who has reached the perfection of humanity, of knowledge or gnosis"). It could also mean "perfect in poetry." This is the longest *ghazal* Mir wrote (twenty-one verses), and not one verse can be viewed as second-rate. He has used twenty-three rhyme words, none of them repeated.

59 Because she went to bathe in the river, the water stopped flowing, either in wonder or because it wanted her reflection to stay in it.

60 Because the beloved had become fashion conscious: he wore a short turban, and that, too, loosely coming down to his forehead in a devil-may-care manner.

61 A favorite theme with poets from classical Persian to classical Urdu, this is a remote allusion to the Qur'anic verse that God offered his knowledge (*amānat,* a trust) to the earth and the skies, but they

refused. Man accepted the burden (see Qur'an, 33:72). The poet emphasizes man's loneliness in the universe.

62   There are many possibile meanings here: because the breeze is going to the beloved's street, but the speaker cannot; because he dreads the news that the breeze may bring forth from there, for the beloved is fickle and cruel; because the speaker wishes to send the beloved a message through the breeze, but is forbidden to do so.

63   In Mir's world, the *shaikh* is also a fool, and gullible. He's being tempted, in two senses: (1) Your going to the tavern would itself be a miracle! (2) If you were to visit a tavern, your spiritual powers would be enhanced and you would do more miracles.

64   Since the Kaaba is a sanctuary, the animals that are let free there are sacrosanct.

65   The conventional wisdom was that madness, especially that caused by love, intensified in the spring. Love-crazed men, like any mad people, were often kept in chains during springtime.

66   Branding oneself on the hands or forearms, or even the thighs, was a way of showing one's intensity of love. A brand or a scar was also called *gul* (rose, flower).

67   Because there were no envelopes in those days for the common man's correspondence, letters before dispatch were twisted into odd shapes—a bird, a twisted strand of cloth, a key—then sealed with the writer's personal seal and handed over to a messenger, who could be a professional letter carrier or a special envoy.

68   This *ghazal* has a rare theme where the speaker is warning the girl (beloved) *against* falling in love with herself, yet the main effect is that of warning her against falling in love with anyone. In this context, see *ghazal* 72 where the protagonist-lover gently chides the beloved for her un–beloved-like ways, which are the result of her falling in love.

69   Because the pen writes, and moves on. There is a lot of wordplay and polysemy going on in this *ghazal*. I have chosen only one interpretation, that which makes most sense in translation.

70   One of the rare *ghazals* in the whole canon addressing a beloved who herself has fallen in love with someone new. It features a little bit of "I told you so" but is much more of a gentle, friendly if somewhat wry summing up of recent events. The speaker's tone is soft, yet decisive. The whole *ghazal* is a triumph of love poetry, though it is love poetry of a singularly different kind. The speaker is certainly a past lover, or aspirant to the girl's favors. Now he's

reconciled to his fate, but still interested enough to open a new chapter in their relationship. In this context, also see *ghazal* 70.

71   The idiom *gurg āshtī* means "hypocritical peace; false peace." Literally, it means "peace of the wolf." In view of the delightful appropriateness of the phrase in the context of the legend (since Joseph's brothers told his father that Joseph had been killed by a wolf), I give a literal translation here.

72   "To drink one's own blood" or "to drink blood" means "to accept a situation with great reluctance, and showing no resistance." Thus the idiom expresses a situation of being totally oppressed.

73   The idea is that the lover's greatest bliss is to be killed by the beloved. In the present case, it's the beloved's sword itself that is ardently desirous of killing the lover.

74   "Infidel" is a word of praise here, delightful in the context of Brahmans and idol houses. *Kāfir* (infidel, rejector [of the true faith]) is a common trope in Urdu and Persian poetry for the beloved, or her attributes. This is because the beloved is supposed to be an enemy, intent on taking the lover's life. And the same convention applies to the infidel: in the *ghazal* world he is an "enemy" of "Islam" and cultivates deadly enmity with the Muslim. The beloved is a *kāfir* because she comes first in all the concerns that a lover may have: before God, before faith, before family. The lover adores, worships the beloved. Thus both step out of their realm of faith: the Hindu becomes *kāfir* in the eyes of the Muslim faith; the Muslim becomes *kāfir* in the eyes of his own faith.

75   (1) To look at her would mean a lack of self-control, giving way to desire, thus showing weakness; (2) the lover is so jealous that he cannot tolerate his own eye looking at the beloved.

76   The idea is that he loves her so much that a mere sight of her face would affect him so strongly that his heart will stop.

77   The speaker insinuates that the boy is no longer good-looking and should accept his advances. In masterly double entendre the poet upholds the convention that the down did not spoil the boy's looks.

78   According to legend, Laila and Majnun never met once their love became known (which was quite early on). So they are amazed at finding themselves together. Stillness is a function of wonder. Since pictures are still by definition, the subject of the painting (and the portrait, obviously) are assumed to be in a state of wonderment.

79   By convention, God is never blamed for any ills or misfortunes. The sky or the skies are a convenient fig leaf. The skies are supposed

176

to be rotating. It is therefore assumed that they do so in search of new mischief, new ways to hurt or to crush or grind to dust the people in the world. In the present instance the poet has created a beautiful conceit: even the sky loves the beloved so much that he is jealous of the pearls in her ears (with which the ear above the lobe was often studded) if they seem to be kissing or competing with her earrings. The implication is not only that even the sky is enamored of her beauty, but also that they are both tyrants, and tyrants love tyrants. The other implication is that the sky, tyrant that he is, does not want anyone to love the beloved.

80 The Urdu and Persian word *āb* means both "water" and "brightness" (as in the English "gem of the first water"). Thus a sharp, bright sword is supposed to be *āb-dar*, "carrying or containing brightness," but since *āb* also means "water," a common simile for the sword is "a water channel, a canal," and if it is a water channel or canal, its water can flow and can also be drunk.

81 A well-known Urdu expression is "scratching one's own face." It is used to express disgust, irritation, dudgeon. See the first verse of *ghazal* 77 for a stronger version of this theme. The interesting thing here is that he is talking of irritation.

82 The heart is a mirror that reflects the image of the loved ones and ultimately even God. A broken mirror can reflect no images.

83 The word in the text is *dandān muzd,* which literally means "remuneration for the teeth." Metaphorically, it means "sweets or goods gifted to the fakirs or dervishes after they have been feasted." But among homosexuals the term meant "a kiss."

84 The original is *mū parīshān,* literally "hair disordered, scattered." When the tresses are not bound or tied, they are called *parīshān*. In Urdu, *parīshān* also means "worried, anxious." *Parīshān* hair thus suggests disorderliness, a tendency to wander around.

85 The rainy season is supposed to be the best time for drinking. Hoping to get drunk, everyone's eyes are dark with "dazzlement." Temporary blindness is often the result when a strong light dazzles the eye. The prospect of getting drunk is so splendidly refulgent that the eyes are dazzled. Though there is little rain in Mecca, the city sometimes suffers serious flash floods. A cloud arising from the precincts of the Kaaba is, metaphorically, a dense, black cloud and full of rain.

86 Sugar, sugar candy, etc., are hygroscopic: they become moist and tend to run when exposed to the air. Hence *shīra nikālnā* means

"the flowing of the treacle" and, metaphorically, "to perspire with shame."

87 The Friday prayer is somewhat more important than the daily five prayers and must be performed in a mosque, behind a prayer leader.

88 Since the water always sits below the bank or shore, the poet creates the conceit that it is full of humility. It chooses a lowly place to sit, even though its clarity shows that it is pure (of heart). More generally: do not underestimate water simply because it sits lower than the bank on which you stand.

89 Aloewood is a valuable incense; it is heavier than water.

90 The pearl is the image of the beloved, or the person of the beloved herself. The Urdu idiom supports both interpretations. The beloved "lives" in the eyes insofar as her image lives in the eyes.

91 Going round someone seven or more times was a way of proclaiming that that person's life should be saved or lengthened in exchange for the life of the one doing the circumambulation.

92 Friday was a holiday as well as a holy day for Muslims. The implications are that (1) Mir starts drinking on Thursday night and perhaps drinks away the whole of Friday, and (2) he comes drunk for the Friday prayer. See also *ghazal* 85, especially the penultimate verse.

93 There is an allusion here to Qur'an 2:115, where God says that his face is everywhere, whichever way you turn.

94 The frame of the mirror is called *khāna,* which also means "home." The mirror cannot leave its home; that is the basis of the conceit here.

95 This is because the yogi wanders from place to place.

96 The prophet Muhammad is known to have favored cleanliness to an extraordinary degree. He recommended the use of an acacia twig, or a twig of some similar tree, called *miswāk* in Arabic (from *saka,* "to rub") to clean the teeth. He commanded people to comb their hair and to bathe frequently.

97 The bulbul is proud because his breast is full of scars too, and the blooming garden is quite like his own scars.

98 "For the rose's sake" is just like "for God's sake."

99 Branding was sometimes resorted to as a "cure" for madness. *Gul,* as we have seen above, means both "rose" and "scar." We have also seen above that scarring one's hands and arms, even the thighs, was considered to be a sign of true love.

100 Because the rose's petals are not closely joined together, that is, they are not seamless. This gives rise to the conceit that, utterly vexed by envy, the rose has torn open its dress.

101 The candle's flame is like a tongue. So long as there is a flame, the candle is alive; but the flame eats away the candle's life, or sometimes a gust of wind may extinguish it. Since the candle flame is like a human tongue, the human tongue is also like a flame. The poet, who always speaks the truth, is punished by beheading or hanging (the reference here could be to the Sufi poet Mansur al-Hallaj). The poet is thus destroyed by his tongue. These are just the obvious meanings. It is difficult to find anywhere else a two-line verse of just fourteen words that can say so much, and so elegantly.

102 Branding was one of the "remedies" for madness in the medieval era. This verse makes use of another medical trope: madness was supposed to become aggravated during the spring. It was also supposed that the scars of branding became darker with the intensity of madness. The suggestion here is that the speaker is in a dark dungeon and cannot see anything outside it but can sense the "brightening" of his scars.

103 The word *'iqd* (used here in conjunction with *suraiya,* Pleiades) means a cluster, a randomly strung necklace, etc. A book of poems is a highly organized work of art; the Pleiades are just a cluster or necklace of pearls randomly put together.

104 Pressing someone's legs was not only a means to take away tiredness or pain in the legs; it was also a token of extreme humility.

105 Short coats and short sleeves were the sign of humility and poverty. Women and affluent people wore their sleeves long. At the sight of her beautiful forearms, the *shaikhs* fell in love and began to rend their garments.

106 The rhyme and the refrain used by the poet in a *ghazal* are known as the *ghazal's zamīn* ("ground, land").

107 *Qalandars* were a type of Sufis or dervishes, in the sense that some Sufis shaved their head, face, and eyebrows to symbolize their freedom from worldly customs and conventions. Some tied a chain around their head to symbolize their mental and spiritual ties to God and no one else, and also to bear the burden like a penance. They were mostly, but not always, itinerant.

108 The *palash* tree loses all its leaves in spring, and is covered with red and orange flowers.

109 A reference to the battle at Karbala (680 C.E.) where the Prophet's

179

grandson Husain and his seventy-odd companions fought Yazid's much superior forces until death. Yazid was the ruling caliph, but Husain and his supporters saw him as a usurper.

110 A slender waist has always been regarded as an important component of beauty. The waist was imagined to be extremely slender, like the veins in a flower petal, or even a strand of hair.

111 "Wine-duck": a wine goblet fashioned in the shape of a duck.

112 "The deer in the Kaaba": nothing, not even an insect, is permitted to be killed in the Kaaba (see n. 64 above). The "cowardly deer of Kaaba," living a life of safety in the Kaaba, is a conceit derived from this custom. Being wounded, or being killed (by the beloved) is life's chief and highest aim. The deer in the Kaaba escapes harm and thus lives a cowardly life.

113 "Blunt pen": *chob-e harfī;* literally, a stick for the letters. Before children were taught writing, they were made to gain acquaintance with the shape of each letter by being made to carefully run a blunt piece of reed-like wood on each letter as written on the practice page or tablet—something like a series of dry runs, which avoided smudging the actual page. This verse is typical of a mode that Mir sometimes adopted: to use arcane meanings of words when the theme of the verse itself is light, if not trite and plain. Here the extremely rare phrase *chob-e harfī* is followed up with *shināsā'ī* to mean "gnosis" and *hisāb* to mean "concern." The meanings are valid, but quite unknown to the average native speaker.

114 The idea is that so long as there is wine, there is springtime.

115 Although medieval Arab science determined that external light and not some source of light in the eye causes things to be seen, Persian and Urdu poetry persist in treating the sight as something that goes out like a ray of light to make the object visible.

116 On doomsday, or the day of resurrection, all the human beings ever born will be gathered on a vast plain, to be judged by God. There will be weeping and wailing and confusion and a general tumult all round.

117 It is a poet's duty, or essential calling, to find new themes for his poems. The poet must grieve for themes that eluded him (that is, slipped his mind before he could "bind" them in a verse), or for themes that just did not come to him. And he should devote his time to the search for new themes, and this concern for new themes should be as oppressive as the sorrow for lost themes. As for other human beings, they should at least have a heart filled with pain,

for to have a suffering heart is to take the first step toward spiritual development. Paper is pale, but does not partake of the meaning of the words written upon it. So mere paleness of the face avails nothing.

118 The sound of the bell penetrates in all four directions while the caravan, and its bell, move on, leaving the sound behind, as it were. This is a favorite trope of Mir's to embody the sense of utter loneliness. Also see *ghazal* 29, verse 5, for the sound of the bell and *ghazal* 93, verse 4, for God's face being everywhere.

119 In the first line *mail-e dil*, "tilt or inclination of the heart," is pronounced indistinguishably from *maile dil*, "dirty heart(s)." And in any case, the word *maile*, "dirty," is a fine pun on the word for "washerman." In the second line, he says *us ko kyā ham dho len hain* ("Do I wash him up?"). Here again the pun is obvious. A naughtier and less obvious pun is that *dho lenā* also means "to sodomize."

120 The Urdu and Persian word for "metrical, within the meter" is *mauzūn*, which means "measured/weighed [and found correct]." Since the beloved's stature is a thing of beauty, it is often described as *mauzūn*, which also means "suitable, proper." A line of verse is *mauzūn*, "metrical." So is the beloved's stature (suitable, proper, and hence measured/weighed [and found correct]). The cypress tree is always straight like a line. Hence the cypress also is *mauzūn*.

121 "Ten days" is used for any small number, but here it also suggests the ten days of mourning in the month of Muharram.

122 The donkey was a normal mode of transport in Arabia, but in India, being made to ride a donkey and taken round in the city is a serious disgrace. "Islami": anyone living in the realm of Islam.

123 See n. 120 above.

124 There is a devilishly untranslatable pun here: (1) If Mir knew about the proprieties of things, he would not do such things; (2) Mir does such things precisely because they are improper.

125 A standard trope for the candle's flame is "tongue." The candle's wick is often trimmed to prevent guttering. Thus the candle had a tongue, but it was cut at some time. "Tongue-cut," *zabān burīda*, is the same as "tongue-tied," but it is also pejorative, signifying one who is at a loss for words or one who has no argument left to support himself in a debate or contest.

126 Mansur al-Hallaj (858–922), mystic and poet of Baghdad, was imprisoned and then executed, some say stoned to death, for his blasphemous utterances, especially of the famous phrase "I am

God." As the emblematic intoxicated lover, he achieved martyrdom and fame because he was totally immersed in the Ultimate Being.

127 The text has *qaid-e 'ibārat* (literally, "confinement, fetters, bondage of the texts"), which remains obscure. Apparently it refers to a practice among the Shi'a Muslims whereby a handwritten paper is placed on the body before burial. This paper contains statutory answers to be given by the dead when questioned in the grave by the angels about his faith. It is called *javāb nāma,* "answer-sheet," or *'ahd nāma,* "covenant."

128 Rustam is the supreme warrior hero of the *Shāhnāma,* the Iranian national epic poem.

GLOSSARY

BAGHAT (literally, "gardens") a neighborhood in Isfahan, Iran, that was well known for its free-living and good-looking young people

bulbul a small greyish bird with a beautiful voice, similar to the nightingale. He sings at night to his beloved, the rose, but his desperate love for her is doomed by the coming of autumn. He shares many of the ordeals, attitudes, and values of the lover

DECCAN the region of central India (which in Mir's day included Gujarat) where Rekhta poetry first developed

FARHAD in Persian story tradition, a humble stone cutter who fell in love with Shirin, wife of Khusrau, and agreed to dig a channel through a stone mountain to bring milk for Shirin's bath. Thus he is also called Kohkan, "Mountain cutter." When he had almost completed the impossible task, he was falsely told that Shirin was dead; he instantly plunged his axe into his own forehead

fakir a wandering Muslim religious mendicant

GABRIEL an angel who often appears as God's special emissary, in connection with the revelation of the Qur'an

JAMSHED a legendary Persian king who owned a magic cup; he could look into it and see everything that was happening in the world

JESUS to Muslims, Jesus was a prophet. He did not die on the cross, but was lifted up by God into the heavens

JOSEPH the Islamic counterpart of the biblical Joseph was one of the prophets; his story is told at length in the Qur'an, Sura 12. In the *ghazal* world he is famous above all for his beauty and belovedness. He is also known for being sold into slavery, and later imprisoned

KAABA the primary pilgrimage center for Muslims, located in Mecca

KHIZR in Islamic folk tradition, a prophet-like figure associated with greenness, fertility, life, and right guidance. He guides those who lose their way, or aids travelers in reaching their destination, or helps those in distress. He is supposed to live in the forests.

Because he found and drank the water of life, he will live till doomsday

KHUSRAU *see* Farhad

LAILA the beloved of Majnun

maidan a town square or esplanade that is the site of public life

MAJNUN in *ghazal* tradition, Qais was the archetypal, "mad" (*majnun*) lover of Laila, who returned his devotion. When she was forcibly married to another, he ran off to the desert, where he was cared for by wild animals who were attracted by his songs about Laila

peri a "fairy"; in Persian story tradition, a beautiful creature made from fire

PILIBHIT a yellow wall. It is also a city almost equidistant from Lucknow and Delhi (160 miles, roughly). Originally named Hafizabad, it has been known as Pilibhit since the late eighteenth century because of a yellow mud wall that reportedly enclosed the city

QAIS *see* Majnun

RAVANA in the Ramayana, the demon-king of Lanka who became infatuated with Rama's wife, Sita, and abducted her—an act that ultimately led to his own death

REKHTA ("mixed, poured, dropped, mixed like mortar for joining") along with "Hindi,"

the name of the Urdu language from the seventeenth to the nineteenth century in Delhi and elsewhere; it also referred to a poem in that language

saqi the "cup bearer"—the beautiful youth who pours out the wine; he is often identified with the beloved

SAYYID an honorary title that denotes a descendent of the prophet Muhammad. Especially after the battle of Karbala (680 C.E.), in which the Prophet's grandson Husain and his seventy-odd companions fought to the death against much superior forces, his descendants laid claim to a legacy of honor and courage

shaikh a stock character in the *ghazal* world; he is ostentatiously and pretentiously pious, but also a fool, and gullible. Mir expresses nothing but disdain for him

SOLOMON in the *ghazal* world, a virtuous king who was the recipient of special powers from God. Among other powers, God gave him a signet ring that controlled demons and permitted speech with animals

SUFI a member of one of the traditional Islamic mystical orders

BIBLIOGRAPHY

Editions and Translations

Mir, Mir Taqi. 1997. *Mir Taqi Mir, Selected Poetry*. Translated by K. C. Kanda. New Delhi: Sterling.

———. 2013a. *Kulliyāt-e Mir.* Vol. 1. 3rd ed. Edited by Zill-e Abbas Abbasi, with additions by Ahmad Mahfuz and Shamsur Rahman Faruqi. New Delhi: National Council for the Promotion of Urdu Language, Government of India.

———. 2013b. *Kulliyāt-e Mir.* Vol. 2. 2nd ed. Edited by Ahmad Mahfuz and Shamsur Rahman Faruqi. New Delhi: National Council for the Promotion of Urdu Language, Government of India.

———. No date. "A Garden of Kashmir: The Urdu Ghazals of Mir Muhammad Taqi Mir." Text and commentary by Shamsur Rahman Faruqi. Translated by Frances Pritchett. Columbia University. http://www.columbia.edu/itc/mealac/pritchett/00garden/project.html.

Other Sources

Ali, Ahmed. 1973. "The Anguished Heart: Mir and the Eighteenth Century." In *The Golden Tradition: An Anthology of Urdu Poetry*, ed. and trans. Ahmed Ali. New York: Columbia University Press, pp. 23–54.

Azad, Muhammad Husain. 1880. *Ab-e Hayat*. Lahore: Azad Book Depot.

———. 2001. *Āb-e hayāt: Shaping the Canon of Urdu Poetry*. Edited and translated by Frances W. Pritchett. New Delhi: Oxford University Press.

Coleridge, Samuel Taylor. 1983. *Biographia Literaria*. Edited by James Engell and Walter Jackson Bate. Princeton, N.J.: Princeton University Press. Original edition, 1817.

Faruqi, Shamsur Rahman. 1999. "Conventions of Love, Love of Conventions: Urdu Love Poetry in the Eighteenth Century." *Annual of Urdu Studies* 14: 3–29.

———. 2001a. "Constructing a Literary Theory, a Canon, and a Theory of Poetry." In *Āb-e hayāt: Shaping the Canon of Urdu Poetry*, ed. and trans. Frances W. Pritchett. New Delhi: Oxford University Press, pp. 19–51.

———. 2001b. *Early Urdu Literary Culture and History.* New Delhi: Oxford University Press.

Lutf, Mirza Ali. 1972. *Gulshan-e Hind.* Edited by 'Ata Kakvi. Patna: Azimush Shan Book Depot.

Mir, Muhammad Taqi. 1972. *Tazkira-ye Nikāt al-Shu'arā.* Edited by Mahmud Ilahi. Delhi: Idara-ye Tasnif.

———. *Remembrances.* 2019. Translated by C. M. Naim. Cambridge, Mass.: Harvard University Press.

Petievich, Carla. 1992. *Assembly of Rivals: Delhi, Lucknow and the Urdu Ghazal.* New Delhi: Manohar.

Pritchett, Frances W. "A Garden of Kashmir." http://www.columbia.edu/itc/mealac/pritchett/00garden/index.html. Retrieved on 9 September 2017.

Russell, Ralph, trans. 2017. *A Thousand Yearnings: A Book of Urdu Poetry and Prose.* Edited by Marion Molteno. New Delhi: Speaking Tiger Books.

Russell, Ralph, and Khurshidul Islam. 1968. *Three Mughal Poets: Mir, Sauda, Mir Hasan.* Cambridge, Mass.: Harvard University Press.

Sauda. 2001. *Divan-e Ghazaliyat-e Sauda.* Edited by Nasim Ahmad. Varanasi: BHU.

Shefta, Navab Mustafa Khan. 1843. *Gulshan-e Bekhar.* Delhi: Urdu Akhbar Press.

Todorov, Tzvetan. 1982. *Symbolism and Interpretation.* Translated by Catherine Porter. Ithaca, N.Y.: Cornell University Press.